DHARMIFY

HARGOBIND KHALSA

DHARMIFY

A DAILY PRACTICE TO GET YOUR MIND RIGHT, YOUR BUSINESS TIGHT, BE A LOVE LIGHT, SO YOU FEEL ALRIGHT

Disclaimer:

The resources in this book are provided for informational purposes only and should not be used to replace professional health, legal, accounting and business advice. Please always consult a trained professional before making any decisions regarding your health and business. The author assumes no liability on behalf of the reader and hopes the work in this book helps you take even more responsibility for your own well being.

I have done my absolute best to tell a truthful autobiographical tale in hopes you see my transformation through dharmify. The lesson I learned retelling stories of the past, is that it is challenging to get a story exactly right. I accept full responsibility for errors that may come about in this text. Please know I did my best to tell it like it was, double checking with others when possible. I have written this with the hope that it is useful to you as the reader. Any mistakes are completely my own.

Dedication

For you Papa Ji,
for doing every seva that ever came your way.

For you Sat Darshan for always riding with me.

For you Mata Ji for showing me what true love is.

DHARMIFY

(verb) to do what matters

(noun) a system to do what matters

Used in a sentence.

How did you know that was the right choice?

I dharmified it.

What is dharmify?

Dharmify is a decision-making system.

Why should you use dharmify?

You can replicate the system and find greater wellness, intimacy, familial bonds, communal relations, make more money, heal yourself, and live with more purpose. Even if you disagree with my system, which you may, you will see that each area of your life should have a system. You can improve upon mine even by rejecting it.

Where does this come from?

I stumbled upon the system through yoga practice, the Sikh faith, building businesses and hustling since I was 14. I think the value of the system lies in its simplicity. You have likely encountered all the concepts before, just not arranged this way. Once you get the hang of dharmify, it is really fast to use.

How long does it take to follow the dharmify process?

Sometimes it can take hours to unpack all the issues, but once you get the hang of it, you can dharmify in 10 minutes or less. I recommend you dharmify daily while trying to keep it to around 20 minutes. Then also use dharmify for major decisions like whether to start a business, how to be a better lover, how to manage your family, flush out issues in a group or how you will heal from a tragedy.

Table of Contents

My story and why this can help you

The logger was salivating like a hunter closing in on his prey. "By the lord's word, I'll be here at 8 AM to start cutting down your trees. First, how about we go out there and shoot one of them bambis between the eyes. Take her home. Saute her up with some onions and garlic. Mhmmm. Finger lickin' good!" As a lifelong vegetarian, I noted how far I had fallen. I looked at the clean cash in his messy truck. I looked to my forest. I looked to my workers that I couldn't pay. They kept moving, oblivious to the quagmire I was in. The logger never cleaned his truck with ripped seats, but he kept his money looking real nice. The guilt put me in my natural slouch like the spirit was sucked out of me. I thought of my carpenter Tim, trying to raise a family on one salary. I looked to George, my electrician, who brought his rate down and extended his terms with me. On the one hand, I was going to miss payroll. On the other hand, I didn't get into this to destroy the Earth. The logger wanted the oak trees and we both knew I couldn't say no. Friends told me the old trees make the pathways so the smaller ones can find their way. I grabbed the stack of crisp $100 bills and muttered weakly, "just the trees".

I was $350,000 over budget. I was three months behind schedule. I was alone in West Virginia with my pride crushed, surrounded by strangers. I hadn't run a million-dollar construction project on 62 acres before and I was reeling from my mistakes.

Lots of guys said I was in over my head. Workers stole my tools. Some took money for work that they never finished. Others did work that wouldn't pass building codes. All the bad work had one thing in common and it was me. I hired every one of them.

Once I started the renovation, it was too dangerous for my daughter, Siana, to live in the project. She and my wife, Siri Om, moved in with my mother-in-law one state away. I realized if I never finished, they would never come back. Our marriage of 10 years was teetering. Siri Om said she couldn't live like this. I used to get mad at her for spending an extra thousand. How mad should she be at me, for spending a million? Truth was, we were out of our money because I spent it all.

One day I took Siana to Taco Bell, conserving the last of my cash. I said, "Do you want one taco or two. She said "Two!" with the excitement of a five-year-old. I said, "Fuck". Our credit cards were maxed. I had $150,000 in credit and owed every penny of it. Three out of my four business bank accounts were negative. My personal account was negative too. My big sister was transferring me money to eat. I was down to our change jar. Paying for things in quarters, nickels and dimes. I despised pennies.

We sold our two Bikram Yoga studios. That started the project. We sold our home and that money lasted a few more months. Siana asked me shortly thereafter, "Why do we have no home?" Still the money wasn't enough. So, we deferred our taxes. Our tax money went into the project. Then the letters began. The Internal Revenue Service alerted the U.S. State Department to revoke our passports until we paid up. That would cut off access to funds from Casa Om Mexico, our first project. The money I was using to float Casa Om Potomac. The rapper Fifty Cent once said Uncle Sam was the biggest gangster on the block and Sam was coming for me.

I had events planned in Mexico. Events that I had already sold. To make money, I had already spent. This is where "good guys" end up "bad guys." I was robbing Peter to pay Paul as many small business owners do. I think a certain percentage of crooks aren't bad per se, they just get in way over their heads. They get in, like I got in. Then they do dumb things out of desperation. My father said sometime later, "It's nice you got to look into the abyss and didn't go into the abyss".

From the outside, you could say I was greedy and ignorant. There's truth to that. Deep down however, I felt something else. I knew the bigger the problem, the better the story if I survived. I was a creator doing it the only way I could. I knew this because I was dharmifying.

I was on a painful path because it was the best choice. The pain I was feeling was the byproduct of growth.

I knew that, somehow, I would fulfill my mission and take care of my obligations.

That is why this book will help you. Because if you deploy the system you will maximize your contribution to every area of your life. So even when things go bad, you know you made the best choices possible. You'll also have a tool to pick yourself up, when you fall.

The seven steps to dharmify are summarized as follows:

Step 1: Soul

Step 2: Karma

Step 3: Dharma (a spiritual path)

Step 4: Vision

Step 5: Chop wood, carry water (the work)

Step 6: Napkin Financials

Step 7: Guru's Blessing (service, luck, alignment and God)

While my position in business and family was painful, I had looked into my soul. I asked myself the hard questions around purpose, faith, and desire. I answered that this was the most meaningful project I could find. It made my soul happy and that's part of Step 1.

I looked at my construction history. I looked at my event planning skills. I looked at my business history. I saw my karma and knew this was a stretch. It was exactly the kind of experience that would yield the seeds of the future for me, my family, and all my clients. I theorized I could build a yoga retreat center outside every major metropolitan city. It was good karma to get which is step 2.

Then I made a business plan. I created an idea based on Step 1 and Step 2. My soul plus my karma equal my dharma and that's step 3.

I looked into the future to see where the retreat center market was going. I looked into the future to see the man I would become by enduring the ordeal. I liked that future version of me. This was my vision and that's step 4.

I reviewed the labor required. I had no idea how much it would take. If I knew it was going to be that hard, I may have never done it. But at the time, I committed to the work. I was game to do whatever it took which is Step 5, chop wood, carry water.

Then I looked to the resources required. I went through the financial calculation. They didn't add up, but it was close enough. The real world is never pretty, and we are never fully ready. From a high level, I reckoned I may never get this close again to a good idea. Step 6, the napkin financials, added up to a yes.

Finally, I looked at who would benefit if I did succeed. I wrote a long list of clients, workers, investors, friends, and family that would love to stay at my yoga retreat center. Summoning to mind this many beneficiaries of my labor made me feel close to God. To be filled with so much confidence and joy, through service to others is to receive the Guru's Blessing and that's Step 7.

You can download the entrepreneur's dharmify at dharmify.com/entreprenuer if you are on the entrepreneur's path.

With these seven steps, I had prepared myself. So as things got bad and the people around me tumbled into pessimism, I had a wholly different, optimistic story unfolding within me. I offer you this system because I want you to have the power to harness your own story as well. I want you to clarify what matters and align your actions to that.

We all need to dharmify. To me, this is everything. You will have more control over your life. You will experience more positive outcomes. You will make better life choices if you have a system. You will feel closer to God. And you can have this every single day.

I was there. I am still there, trying to figure it out. What I discovered was a process. Your parents, religion, the media, culture, marketing... they will sell you answers. Do this. Believe that. Buy these.

Dharmify is the opposite. Dharmify is not offering you answers, it is offering you questions to be asked in a special sequence. The process then activates the spiritual, material, aspirational and practical aspects of yourself. Once answered, dharmify then works as an interactive map and guide for the topic of your choice. There are no right answers, just your answers. You can be religious or listen to your parents or seek shortcuts on the internet. But with dharmify, you will own the choices and everyone else's suggestions will funnel more consciously through your lens.

Dharmify also works as a protective shield. It will help you say "no" to the infinite distractions we all encounter. At any given moment you will have the tools to make the best choice. Not to say I don't still make mistakes. I do. But they are new mistakes informed with the lessons of my past karma, my soul, and with thought for my dharma and the future. Follow the system and you'll be there too.

Dharmify will help with your choices but it is also a way to harmonize the past and future, to reflect and grow. Through this, I will share my story and tell you about what happened to me when I deviated from this path. I will tell you about my business failures, the dangerous encounters and my self-destructive choices. The marital and family risks with hopes that this will be helpful to you. This is just the system I created to simplify the wisdom and use it in a structured way.

To me, the goals of health, intimate relationships, family, community, and business follow a similar pattern. The system can be deployed in each of the areas. As I build micro-wins in the area of my work, my expressions in the real world get more profitable, powerful and satisfying. I get to ride upward spirals, the juice behind dharmify. We will get into a step-by-step guide for upward spirals at the end of the book.

The purpose of sharing my story is to make a connection. I am trying to make you feel something by witnessing my vulnerabilities, shame, recklessness, and mistakes. Evoking emotion brings the energy to make positive change. In poker, as in sex, they say you got to give action to get action. The advanced poker player will always lose a few big hands at first to loosen up everyone at the table, so the bets get bigger.

Let's go back in time, and I will tell you more about me. I was born in the United States but went to boarding school in Amritsar, India when I was 12. My parents insisted it wasn't a punishment, but I had just been suspended from my nice American private school. I had been building so much resentment and we all agreed it would be a fresh start. I was so excited to be free.

Unfortunately, the boarding school was dissolving like a failed colonial outpost. Corruption was rampant. Administrators were stealing money. The school accountant was running a kickback scheme that became notorious in the streets of Amritsar. Cleaning staff were stealing supplies - the cleaning lady even had a scam going where she would steal the brooms and resell them in the market. The dining hall administrator fabricated a visa renewal scam. Half way through the year, he collected a fee from each foreigner like me to pay the Indian government to renew our visas. Except, he never paid the government and there was never really a fee. Turnover was constant and we the students were going buck wild. Discipline was often harsh and physical abuse was common. I went from out of control in America to out of control in India.

Back then in 1995, Amritsar was in a massive transition of its own. It was recovering from military rule. The Sikhs tried to break from India in 1984 to form their own separate country called Khalistan. It failed. The movement was put down with violent repression. It seemed all of our neighbors had someone missing or murdered from their family. One of our staff members walked with a limp because he had grenade shrapnel in his leg. Supposedly, he got the school job after getting fired from the Golden Temple for stealing 40 tubs of Ghee. When I met people that lived through the uprising, I wondered who they had betrayed to survive.

India as a whole was also undergoing its own transformation. In his book *India Unbound*, the author Gurcharan Das, calls this period the "rebirth of a dream." It was a great time to see India grow. Still saddled by its socialist "license raj" economic system, bribery, corruption and inefficiency were everywhere. India post-independence had so much hope only to be saddled with the devils of despair: lack of opportunity and poverty. The strict, socialist bureaucratic system was slowly loosening by the 90's but it was still messy. A police officer tried to pressure me into a bribe one time mostly for being white. I was studying fast as I watched a kid two years older than me negotiate the price down. Another time, a few cops were getting drunk next to us at Sharma Dhaba on Ranjit Avenue. A friend convinced the tipsy cop to let him play with his gun. Eventually a supervisor reprimanded him and us, extolling the virtues of gun safety in a slurred voice as his comrades laughed along with us.

When the systems fail, the characters come alive. As the structures fell apart, I got wild.

Emboldened every day, I broke every rule I could. First, I started smoking. I learned to roll paper tobacco and later smoked cheap cigarettes called *bidis*. Then I started drinking alcohol. I used to buy Godfather beer from a blind man. I started eating meat, which was a real taboo in my culture. I tried butter chicken but didn't fall in love. I got into fights with bigger and older students. I developed a three-part attack which I practiced over and over again. It included a stunning slap to the face, a knee to the head and then a head lock to hopefully knock them out. I was so proud when I choked a student 2 years older than me until he submitted. My practice paid off. I have an inch-long scar on my right knee from a powerful strike I once landed in someone's face.

One time I was throwing firecrackers out the dorm window. We called them bombs. They were small packs of gunpowder we rolled by hand for extra pop. I had my afro out and I used the wick to light it on fire. I thought what's better than throwing firecrackers out of the window? Throwing firecrackers with your head on fire! For most, that's crazy. For Sikhs who aren't supposed to cut their hair, that's blasphemy with insanity.

Once on the way to class, I broke my teacher's window just to see it fall. I used my nonchalant side-arm technique to launch a bottle of Spike seasoning I had stolen. The glass bottle was just light enough to be discreet and just strong enough to break the pane. And then someone snitched, and I landed straight in a Punjab Police jail cell with 5 other grown men. We all shared one blanket on the floor. It was soaked in sweat and piss and looked like it had been there since before India's independence 50 years earlier. I stood for hours ready to fight to make sure I wasn't going to get raped as I sized up my cell mates. I was grateful to have my black hoodie on so that when I laid down, I didn't have to touch my face in the filth. The toilet was a hole behind an eighteen-inch brick wall. Relieving myself with 5 strangers watching is some memorable shit.

The head of the prison had the same name as my dad, Satwant Singh. I figured he tortured people, but I can only imagine his confusion when I landed there. He made me write over-and-over that I was sorry like Bart does in the opening credits of *The Simpsons*. He was impressed that I could read and write in Punjabi.

Physically, I got released from jail. Mentally, I was still the same kid. But my luck was running out. The path of destruction caught up with me as karma sometimes does.

In India, the best seat on the bus is on the roof. Generally, when all the seats inside are taken, people ride on the luggage racks on top. It was my favorite spot. One night while no one was watching, I climbed out the side of the bus as it was barreling down the road. We were going unusually fast which made it even more fun. I imagined the bus was trying to launch me, but I was a more skilled surfer.

I grabbed the metal roof top luggage rack and stood on the windowsill. The wind blew in my face as I rode the metal wave. I looked ahead into the darkness and then pulled myself to the roof. I loved the feel of the thick, hot breeze in Punjab Spring. I loved to stare at the stars between the clouds. I would cross my hands behind my head and my feet at my ankles. I was a free boy.

The rules did not apply to me, right up until they did. As I sat up briefly, I was blindsided by an electric cable smashing me straight in the head. Taking the strike face first, the cable ripped out four teeth, including my canine on the right side. It broke the maxilla bone in my mouth and burned my right cheek.

As blood exploded from my head, my neck cocked back. I wondered: perhaps this is the end? I had been punched in the face many times, but nothing like this. It was so much more vicious, as if all punches before had been pulled.

I was fortunate that my head wasn't taken clean off. Any higher, it may have blinded me. Any lower, it would have decapitated me. A dentist later said, he had never seen the full, inch long canine come out of someone still living.

Later, I had the tooth dipped in silver like the Nihang warriors did and someone stole it at Nanak Nivas. If you read this and happen to know where it is, please call me and I will give you a cash reward.

The impact disfigured my two front teeth, so they stuck out face forward for my lip to rest upon softly. I rolled onto my back. I laid down in my thick crimson blood and waited for the bus to stop. I remember the stars sparkling as if calling me home. The driver saw what happened and fled. In India, if something goes wrong, the driver always gets blamed. So, he fled with my teeth on top. That's how it was back then. In shock, I thought I was ok. Fine in fact, until I saw the horror in the mirror. One of my best friends, Satbir, says I then started screaming and punching myself in the face to try to reset the teeth. He was right behind me on the bus and it has haunted him since. He and others then subdued me until I stopped. Other people saw the hideousness and looked away. Then, they had to look back to see more. I underwent surgery for hours to repair my face. The dentist made a crude brace that reset some of my teeth. I later got punched in the face and the brace gashed into my upper lip tissue. Each time I moved my cheeks after that, the brace would reattach to my open flesh wound shooting sensations of pain to my brain. It forced me to keep a face with puckered lips like the models in Zoolander for days.

I couldn't eat solid foods for months. Everything I ate came out of the blender. My favorite food was blended mashed potatoes and gravy. It dawned on me: maybe I am going to die doing this stuff. I wasn't sure I cared. A few weeks later, I took a high dose of ground nutmeg in a smoothie to get fucked up. I remember the floor starting to spin. I got so high I passed out in a cold, tiled bathroom. When I came back, it was as if I exited the ceiling to a world still spinning. Eventually I got up. I went to eat something, and I realized I couldn't chew. I couldn't smile. I was alone and drugged up. I wasn't sure how long I remained out on the floor, but it was probably hours. There was no one coming to save me. If I wanted out, I better get out. It was a soul moment. I touched the bottom but not like I would later. I was 13.

The year before, I had traveled to India to learn meditation, yoga and Sikh religious practices. My parents were devotees of the Indian yoga master, Yogi Bhajan. I was raised Sikh. But with my white skin, Jew fro, and sloppy turban, I was an alien in America. Kids used to call me diaper head at the mall, condom head at Kings Dominion, a girl at the pool, and my nickname at basketball camp was the "man from Pakistan". Boys used to whistle at me when we played shirts vs skins and threaten to cut all my hair off in celebration.

I was 7 the first time I had to stand up to security in a bathroom while arguing that I was a boy. Coming back from camp, I got left at the Albuquerque airport for 6 or 7 hours. I had broken my arm rollerblading on a halfpipe. The doctor wrapped my arm from wrist to bicep in a red fiberglass cast. I was so upset because it meant I couldn't reach my head to tie my turban and keep my wild hair out of my face. I wandered the small airport going back and forth pondering what to do for hours.

So, I went to the bathroom to use the mirror to get my afro tied back with just one arm. One adult after another harassed me for being a girl in the men's room until someone called security to kick me out as they did at numerous pools. I resolved to not leave, even spinning in circles to get an angle on my head and turban. I told the security guard that I was a boy, and I wasn't leaving. Not convinced, I asked if he wanted me in the ladies room instead. We eventually reached detente and he left me to struggle on my own.

More time passed. Eventually, a stranger helped me. He said his daughter also broke her arm and he could relate. So, between our three arms we did something. It looked absolutely ridiculous, but my hair was out of my face. I remember thinking most people are bad but sometimes a good one appears if you stick it out. I later saw the UNICEF social experiment with the child Anano where strangers treat her poorly based on her messy look. I couldn't agree more with that observation of human nature.

By my account I had a privileged upbringing. My parents always put my sister and me first. But it was volatile. In a short period, my father lost his job, we had our car repossessed and fell behind on our bills. I went to the principal's office of my private school and they let me know my parents were late on payments. The powerlessness and burden I felt at this time directly led to my rage towards authority and commitment to entrepreneurism. Falling out of the middle class is a crushing experience. For the reasons mentioned, I detested America.

In India, I was even more unusual. With my blue eyes and American swagger, I was so obviously an *angreji*, a foreigner. The white skin in India came with the perception of wealth, so people used to target me to steal my stuff. I got hit by pickpockets, shoe thieves, and baggage lifters.

Three Nihangs mugged me one time. I was traveling solo at the train station in Delhi. They surrounded me and one asked for *Baksheesh* showing me a rip in his clothing. Baksheesh generally is a blessing from a temple. In this case, I was the blessing. I told them to go to *gurdwara* when one grabbed me. I pulled away and a second one punched me as I shoved back. I then fled into traffic and got hit by a motor rickshaw. I bounced away with a few scratches and fled down a back alley. India wasn't my country either.

Eventually it dawned on me that the one thing these locations had in common was me. I could play the hand I was given and make it worse. Or I could play the hand I was dealt and make it better. I could dharmify.

One day, I went to the Darbar Sahib also known as the Golden Temple. I never loved the inside. The inside felt like it was for people who had achieved something. Outside it felt like the most spiritual place on Earth for those who hadn't done anything.

I sat down on the cold marble surrounding the temple. In my Indian *kurta* and *kacheras* my shins connected to the cold. It was just cold enough to make you present. I closed my eyes with force. The first time I meditated, it was like hell was unleashed inside me. I could see the reflection of light bounce back on my closed eyelids. I really meditated like my life depended on it because it did. The lesson I took away was that everyone can kill themselves. Everyone can break stuff. Everyone can be a hater. But it is very special to build and improve upon what we have.

Dharmify started here.

I started building. I built a business.

At boarding school, I began buying and selling biscuits, cookies, juices, ice cream and more. Over three years, a friend and I built our operation from the trunk in my dorm into a thriving business with a pool table, freezers, refrigerators, a fish tank, and a full-on lounge. It was called the Caf, a common Punjabi word for a cafeteria. I got to know the streets of Amritsar through commerce. There was the wholesale market and that was my favorite. It was supposed to be for only business owners where goods could be bought at below the MSRP, Manufacturer's Suggested Retail Price. I loved it when I convinced the vendors that I too at 14, had a business. I opened a wholesale account. No matter where I went, I was an outsider. But in the marketplace, I made it inside. I was a *caf walla.*

I would use my day off from school to fill up a cycle rickshaw with goods to sell throughout the week. While everyone else was going for a special dinner in town or playing video games, I was roaming the streets for things to sell. I would lay all my goods out on a table for sale and make up prices. At first, I did a deal with the Coke Company. They didn't take me seriously, so they just gave me a plastic box. It would hold ice and 300 milliliter bottles of Coca Cola. Every 4 days, I arranged a giant block of ice to arrive on a cycle rickshaw. I would break it up and put it in the container to keep drinks cold. When they saw how much I could sell, they gave me the nicest fridge with a blazing red Coke sign. I was so proud. I found a French bakery called La Patisserie that would make cinnamon rolls and croissants. I cut a deal with Quality Walls. They gave me a freezer and I went into the ice cream business. Sandeep, my sales rep, told me I became the second largest seller of his ice cream in all of Amritsar. His only bigger client was Novelty, an iconic shop on Lawrence Road, just adjacent the famed Grand Trunk Road.

As Gurcharan Das said, if the 90's was "a rebirth of the Indian dream", it took me along with it.

The Grand Trunk road runs from Kolkata to Kabul passing through Amritsar and runs West through Chheharta where I lived. It is one of the oldest roads in Asia and was built by emperors and traders thousands of years ago. It is mentioned in the Mahabharata. Rudyard Kipling described it like this: *"Look! Look again. And chumars, bankers and tinkers, barbers and bunnias, pilgrims – and potters – all the world going and coming. It is to me as a river from which I am withdrawn like a log after a flood. And truly the Grand Trunk Road is a wonderful spectacle. It runs straight, bearing without crowding India's traffic for fifteen hundred miles – such a river of life as nowhere else exists in the world."*

We called it GT road and I was sad to learn it wasn't short for Golden Temple Road. The temple was the center of my world for a period and I couldn't imagine Grand Trunk Road predating it. Amritsar is called a Holy City, but without the Grand Trunk road, you would never get there. I rode that highway by bus and hung off the side of yellow and black motor rickshaws as I searched for goods. I had a purpose for the first time. GT road, like the traders of the past, was taking me there. Commerce paved the way for the temple.

Before I opened my shop, I was greatly influenced by a shopkeeper named Bobby. I bought a pack of milk from him one day. Milk was a luxury. Simultaneously, he gave away a sweet to a poorer boy who ran up to him with a big smile. I asked him why he didn't give me one and he said, "I charge you for milk so I can give sweets to the poor kid."

Another time my friend Pankaj, who also owned a shop, took me to the dhaba. He was the most prosperous and savvy of my neighbors at Ranjit Avenue. I asked him, "What's the difference between giving me a coke at the store, when you pay for me at the dhaba?" He explained to never disrespect your business by giving it away. Charge a premium in your store so you can be generous outside your business. I loved these lessons and I aspired to be like Bobby and Pankaj when I later started my first business.

By the end of high school, my business partner and I were employing five people and living large in the Punjab. Vendors would come visit me at school. I would get special permission to skip out on class for business meetings. Our school shifted from downtown Amritsar to the outskirts near the Pakistan border. That's where I opened. The remote location gave me a near monopoly on sales. Eventually, I was making more money than my teachers. Resentments boiled among the Administration. They would have to come get me when the Coke guy showed up or the ice cream man arrived in his new Tata SUV. I was getting too successful.

In India, school was paying me. For a kid that resented authority, this was the fight I was made for. There were discussions of how much electricity I was using. I got word that the cost of my independent operation was burdening the school.

It came down to power in real and imagined ways. The decree came that we could only open in very restrictive hours. It would make the business unsustainable. I had perishable goods I had to sell. I had equipment that I had to pay for.

I used my profits to bribe my little homies to skip school and sneak out to the city. I created a security nightmare by sending students in as many directions as possible. Two dusty roads went to town through fields of mustard greens. Behind the dining hall was a dusty brick wall. I sent others to scale it as they fled the school grounds. I sent groups in three directions causing utter chaos. Then I waited. Shortly thereafter, the Administration came to me and said the students need a fun place to gather. I could help them. If we worked together to improve my store, there would be less incentive to ditch to town. My store hours were restored after that. I paid my peers to not ditch for a while so things would calm down.

My dad later said, "I sent you to India to find enlightenment and instead you opened a 7-11." It's not that I wasn't interested in Indian spirituality. I was. I was just crippled with a debilitating sense of being a fake American, disingenuous Indian and lost immigrant. I was hurt, failing and careless. I started here. I realized I wanted out of my own traps. So, I began to deconstruct my karma and leverage it. And I needed some new teeth.

Years later, my wife, Siri Om and I opened a beach hotel in Mexico. The first Casa Om. We purchased a failed yoga retreat center and remodeled it. Only when one of my contractors asked if I was *mojado*, a wetback, did I realize what I was. I went to Mexico and began a major construction project. Many Mexicans journey North across the frontier to find opportunity. Here I was doing the reverse migration. I was going to another new country to make a better life for myself.

I spent nine months learning the towns of Cancun, Playa Del Carmen and Puerto Morelos through the eyes of lower middle class construction workers. Just like how I got to know Amritsar. I aspired to learn construction like my Mexican co-workers. The concrete buildings and marble reminded me of Punjab. The basic food staples of beans and rice brought me back. Family cohesion and kindness of the people also felt familiar. I fell in love with Mexico. Like India, it felt like home. But it was a challenge. I struggled to learn Spanish and adapt to the culture. Once again, the police would love to extort money from me, the foreigner.

Sometimes I think of myself as a beautiful cow waiting to get milked. Cops routinely call me Bin Laden in Mexico to which I either correct them as "No, no, Saddam." Or I hit them with my Bin Laden. I point my fingers like machine guns while making a *ch ch ch* sound and curse in Punjabi. It, without fail, leaves them in stitches. On the day of my Casa Om Potomac inspection, I did this impersonation for the Fire Marshal in West Virginia. I have never seen authority approve permits so quickly. We are all not so different after all.

I came to Mexico well prepared on many levels. But I had so much to learn. I was given some advice when I first arrived. The storyteller called himself a shaman. I think that meant he could sell me *ayahuasca,* the holy man drug of choice. He told me a tale of an American and a Mexican.

They go into business together. They form a construction partnership. They purchase land together and then seek investment. They go to an investment group in Mexico City and present three proposals. The first idea is to build condos. They suggest a 50-50 split with profits distributed evenly. Construction would begin immediately.

The investors say, "Maybe. What else do you have?" The partners continue, "We can develop the land and sell it to a grocery store". The investors reply again, "Maybe. What else?" The partners present the last idea. They will develop a mix of commercial and residential units. Once again splitting profits 50-50 with the investors.

Hearing the split, the investors hesitate and say, "No. This is no good". The meeting ends. The investors thank the builders and depart.

The partners leave the meeting and share their reflections. The Mexican is clearly upset. The American is more hopeful.

The American says, "Why do you look so sad?" The Mexican says, "Well, what did you hear?" The American says, "The first two ideas had promise. They said maybe. The third one, they didn't like. They said no. You can't win them all. Let's wait and see what they come back with."

The Mexican looked gaunt. He continued, "Let me explain something. When a Mexican says yes, he means maybe. When he says maybe, he means no. When he says no, he means go fuck yourself."

The shaman, seeing my youth and inexperience, then asked if I needed his help. I said "no" and we laughed because we both knew, I did. He gave me his blessing with a smile. Eventually Casa Om Mexico grew into the most frequented hot yoga retreat center in the world.

Years later, I moved to West Virginia to build Casa Om Potomac. One of my contractors reminded me that, "it's a good ol' boy network up here and you're not a good ol' boy". My neighbor caught me at the mailbox one day. My strategy was to be a ghost and get my retreat center open before anyone pinned me as the next Wild Wild Country. He rolled up in a four-wheeler with a giant "Eat Beef" license plate. He asked where I was from. I said with a smile, "Virginia." He said, "It's ok. We won't hold it against you". I was relieved to hear West Virginians make fun of everyone else, too. My mantra at the time was, "piglets get cuddled, but hogs get slaughtered" and I would keep my head down in West Virginia. On my first visit to Lowes, a guy in the plumbing department hollered, "Motherfucker, what's on your head?" I had karma in West Virginia and I better be careful.

Six months into construction, I was out digging a gas line in front of the house. It was early morning, and I was already sweating as I dug with my shovel and digging bar. A sea container delivery man rolled up with a flatbed truck. With the confidence of a local he said, "Yoga retreat center. Ha! Never gonna happen. Lived here all my life. No one does yoga. No one wants yoga. Never going to work." Intrigued, I asked why he felt so strongly about this. He continued to list all the reasons it would fail. He reveled at the sight of another fool blowing his money on a misunderstanding of the market. Sweat ran down my back. I stomped my shovel to the earth to keep moving. Always keep moving in construction. Finally, he asked, "Well, who are you"? I admitted, "I am the owner."

It didn't faze me because I had visioned it already. He couldn't see what I saw. I thought, I am going to stick this guy in my book. Because one day his doubt would be so funny. I just had to keep digging. I call it chop wood, carry water.

Late one evening, a few months into the project, one of my subcontractors came over. It was dark and power was cut to some areas. The project was a mess. There was drywall debris everywhere. Dust was in the air. I made peanut butter and jelly sandwiches as we got to chatting.

He said, "You know Hargobiiind, most of the people that come up this way to build their mansions from DC, they think they are better than us. Lawyers, lobbyists, rich people. They want a West Virginia getaway. They kind of talk down to us, you know, like we're below them. But you, Hargobiiind, you're not like that. You could be a redneck just like me."

Ironically, the main mansion at Casa Om Potomac was constructed by a D.C. lawyer by the name of Charles Cox. He came from a family of lawyers going back to Reconstruction. His grandfather defended Andrew Johnson in his impeachment trial before the US Supreme Court. His brother Archibald Cox was fired by President Richard Nixon in what became known as the Saturday Night Massacre. Archibald's firing is considered the first shot that then brought down Nixon's presidency. Archibald would later write his memoirs in our library. I love that I could buy a rich man's mansion and open it to the public for yoga retreats.

The afro turban wearing Mexican shopkeeper from India just had to become a redneck first. This is where dharmify took me.

The culmination of these experiences across the world formed the process for this book. Languages were different, cultures varied, currencies changed -- but the steps were the same. When I deviated from this path, things in my life were very painful. In fact, I committed to the process after making major mistakes in each of the seven areas.

Here's my guarantee. If you follow the system, you will always know that you made the best possible choices. I am not overselling here. Let me make this clear: Dharmify is no guarantee of victory. The unknown is factored into Guru's Blessing.

Things can and sometimes do go south. We are facing imminent death and disaster, always. We are flying through the universe at 1000 miles an hour on a rock circulating an explosive massive ball of fire. We all know how all our stories end. I cannot solve this for you or me. However, with dharmify, you will know you did the best that you could with the short precious time you have. I am confident this system will add value for anyone, anywhere.

However, the few million dollars I have made and my success in my business are not where the bragging rights are. Lots of people have done better. My accomplishment is that I clarified what mattered to me and I have been doing that over and over again.

The lasting accomplishment is that I can do things my way in spaces that are meaningful. I can succeed in multiple countries looking the way I look. I have done this while keeping my family together. Above all, the process has been hugely satisfying and I have had a positive impact on those around me.

People told me I would never survive in Mexico. That the drug cartel would kill me. A Mexican told me I should pretend to be Jewish because the cartels in Mexico are afraid of Israelis. In West Virginia, people said to be careful because the rednecks will push out a turban wearing Sikh. They said the fanatic Christians would never support a yoga retreat center. People told me India was the most corrupt country on earth. I would never be able to build a business there. In each location, I kept adding up the lessons and refining the system. Instead of being scared, I saw the new places as a chance to grow and test my skills.

There is nothing new here. It is just organized in a unique and practical way. Dharmify started first as an entrepreneurial system. Ironically, the principles all come from yoga and Sikh philosophy except one. Napkin Financials come from accounting. As I mentioned, I used them to build businesses in India, Mexico, and the United States. I used them to build community through the festivals I co-founded, One Fire Hot Yoga Festival and Sat Nam Fest. I used them to start a beach clean-up in Mexico. I used them to navigate through the building and selling of Bikram Fairfax and Bikram Bethesda to publicly traded Yoga Works Inc. I used them to build our retreat centers, Casa Om Mexico, and Casa Om Potomac.

Then I found it to be super helpful in the other areas of my life.

I now use it regularly to improve my marriage by focusing on what I can do. I started aligning my vision for a great relationship with the work I am going to put in. I am glad to have had this tool, or I definitely would have taken my business and health goals too far and neglected my family. More about this later.

I am certainly a performance motivated person but don't get lost in that. The process is a mirror. There are no right answers until you decide they are right. There are no explicit goals unless you want goals. Sometimes, the answer is stop setting goals. If there is a main purpose, it's contentment. As Buddha said, "Contentment is the greatest wealth." The process is personal reflection. This isn't dogma. What you believe is irrelevant. It's not a religion, though I borrowed from religion. It's all about what you do. This will just help you reflect and grow in your unique way.

The system is a balance between inner and outer work, inspired in part by my name.

I was named after the 17th century warrior, Guru Hargobind from India. Many years ago, I did an exchange program in Argentina. When I arrived at my host family's home in Rosario, I introduced myself. The host father rolled his eyes and cocked his neck like I burdened him with a heavy weight. Unique names come with karma. In fact, I estimate that I will spend about 2 months of my life spelling my name if I live until 80. He said, "Por favor, no" like only the Argentinians can. He continued that it's impossible to have such a difficult name. He insisted on calling me Nacho. I implored, "Please, not Nacho." He continued, "Fine. We will name you Tito." And so, it was. At the tender age of 21, I was christened. In South America, I was known as Tito. A few weeks into my stay, my host mom approached me. She said, "I just want to apologize for being so rude on the first day of your arrival." I said," No, of course not. You all are great." She continued, "It's just, when we saw your name, we were hoping for a real Indian".

I love my real name though. The Guru was famous for wearing two swords. He named them, as some lovers of weapons do. The first was named Miri. It was to represent the external struggle in the world. The second was named Piri. It was to represent the internal struggle. Guru Hargobind fought in many battles but struggled for spiritual transformation. In a similar fashion, I hope you can use this book to win the battle inside. We cover this in the first two steps. Then we build confidence for how to create things on the outside in the last 4 steps. Dharma is the present moment. This is my interpretation of the meaning behind Guru Hargobind's Miri and Piri.

Dharmify may create contentment with where you are now. Sometimes I do the dharmify process and feel so happy about my choices. Sometimes I do it and feel tremendous discontent. Then, I can build a plan to control as much as I can control. I do these steps over and over for my business, marriage, family, habits, and community. **If it's important to you, dharmify it.** Each time I can look back in the previous notes to see how I have changed and to track the progress I am making with what's important. That's also fascinating to me. The documents show me how much I have changed in the years since I started doing this. I have changed a lot. I would not have seen how much if I didn't have a record of it.

Let's get into it.

The first two steps represent the past. They represent where you are from and will build the foundation for what is meaningful.

CHAPTER ONE:
SOUL

Noun: the spiritual or immaterial part of a human being or animal, regarded as immortal.

Do the soul work day and night, (and you will) see the divine light deep within.

Siri Guru Granth Sahib Page 1039

"Mr. H! We had no idea you were home!" Many months in and they still hadn't learned my name. But here they were, having a blast without me and, well, on me. The excavation team had brought golf clubs to work. They were using the driver to smash golf balls into the Potomac. While the excavator sat, the skid steer idled and the dollars burned, Big Bertha was powering shots into the river.

Most days it was like running a frat house. I called it entrepreneur's *Survivor*. I kept thinking, if I survive in West Virginia before everyone takes my money, I'd get a million dollars. Except, there was no one to give me a million dollars. The workers boarded up the door of what would become room 10. I kicked in the 5/8ths plywood with my yellow steel toe boots, just for effect. Fear ran over their faces. Then we all realized there were three of them and just me.

So, I started driving golf balls into the river, too, because Tito would have to become a good ol' boy to survive this one.

I wondered many times, "why?" I could have been in Mexico sipping smoothies on the beach. I could have been kite surfing at Playa Mujeres or scuba diving at Casa Om Mexico. I could have been swimming in Cenotes, the ancient underwater caves of the Mayan Riviera. I already won there.

Unbeknownst to me, it turned out there were ancient limestone caves on the new property, too. Three months into construction a lady came over and explained there were sacred Indian caves under the foundation of the house. The seller didn't tell me that one. It was called Indian River Cave. What were the chances that the shopkeeper from **the real** India would come to own Indian caves in West Virginia? The Opequan tribe used the land as a trading post and the cave to store their dry goods hundreds of years ago. Later, a young George Washington surveyed the land and took ownership of it as payment before selling it on.

The answers kept coming. I had soul in this. It was my journey and artistic contribution to the universe. And deep down, I loved every single minute of it. It was an adventure of my own making. I imagine at one point the prosperous Indian traders of the past and a young President Washington too, arrived here full of wonder and curiosity. I was now in their footsteps.

I don't believe in a soul, per se. The idea that there is a little spiritual creature inside of us that floats around and reincarnates or goes to heaven. I have no reason to believe that it happens in that order. I think it was a revolutionary concept once upon a time. Even though the word "soul" is imprecise, it carries the most meaning for me. I think it's useful.

I call "soul" a mix of the curiosity, emotions, desires, purpose, and love that we all have. It's a category of energy. All the dharmify steps are categories where we put important ideas about ourselves. Great ideas have so much soul. Love and passion and kindness and great performance is done with so much soul. The soul is full of goodness on so many levels. Casa Om Potomac felt that way when it started. But it's been a long time coming. There were layers to the soul. I will tell you the story about it.

In the Fall of 2007, my team and I rented a large campground in West Virginia for Sat Nam Fest, a yoga and music festival. We called it Spirit Fest back then. The camp was beautiful but run down and poorly managed. The owner was a savage businessman. Just before the first meal, he came to us and said I had to pay more than we agreed in the contract, or he would not serve the menu we confirmed. He waited until our 200 plus guests had already arrived before he pounced. In dramatic fashion, he went so far as barring his own staff from the kitchen with a chain and lock bolt until more money arrived. It was a showdown and he was ready to go all the way. I was young and naive and afraid that my first major event would end in disaster. I literally didn't have the money though either. When you build a festival, it starts as an idea in your head. Then you share it with someone. Then you build a team. Then you sell it to a few hundred people. It takes a year and so many hours of hard work and you usually lose money. So you can imagine my pain when someone was going to ruin what I had worked for. Trapped, I agreed to pay more, before the clients ever knew what happened. I post dated a check and handed it over. Extortion is a strong negotiating position.

The experience left me with a searing impression. If the operator could build a facility with poor customer service, organization, maintenance, and ethics, just imagine what would happen with efficiency, legendary service and an obsession with quality. It left me with the thought that one day, I would do it better.

But building in America is expensive and hard. There is little room to learn as you go. So, I went for it in Mexico first. We built Casa Om in Puerto Morelos. It was named after Siri Om. It was going to be like her. It was unpretentious and beautiful and meant to inspire authentic yoga practice. Still the memory lingered. We had karma left in West Virginia. My karma often takes me through India.

It is hard to know which ideas come first. It is hard to know how many ideas converging together make a good idea. But good ideas have lots of legs to stand on. That's how I knew my thinking was good. That's how I knew there was soul in it.

I wanted a reason to go back to India. That was first. I wanted to build a West Virginia retreat center. That was second. I wanted to show people India the way I love India and that was third.

I wanted to go to the factories that make the Rajasthani Indian furniture. That was fourth. I wanted to show my daughter India, so she has that connection. That was fifth. Soul has so much energy in it.

I had all these ideas, but I couldn't do just one of them. They wouldn't have worked on their own or they would have been prohibitively expensive.

So, I did them all. It took time. But the end products were so much better. They had purpose, vision, and layers.

Eight months in advance, Siri Om and I planned the India trip. Two weeks before we left, we bought the fixer upper that would become Casa Om Potomac. Then we set off. We went to New York and picked up our friends Jared and Tony. With a stop in Moscow, we headed for Hindustan. We took 25 people with us through Rishikesh, Amritsar, Dharamsala, Delhi and Agra. We promoted it as a yatra, a spiritual pilgrimage. I showed the group all the places I loved to explore as a wild teenager. We meditated with Buddhist monks, did yoga with Himalayan swamis, and chanted kirtan with classical Indian music masters. We explored the spiritual sites from Sikhism, Islam, Buddhism and Hinduism. That alone would have been the trip of a lifetime. But we were just warming up.

After 14 days of entertaining a group of newbies to India, we dropped them at Indira Gandhi Airport. They went home with epic memories.

Our next job began. We went to the desert in Jodhpur. It's the antique furniture capital of India. Our hosts made their livelihoods in the rubble of India's industrialization. While I was breaking windows in the 90's, they were building their fortunes. They would go into the old neighborhoods getting torn down to make way for India's urbanization. Prior to demolition, they would strip the old buildings of iron work, and hand carved furniture, creating an antique collectors dream. By the time I arrived, they had a furniture replica factory and store house the size of 8 Walmarts. It was jam packed stuffed with hand carved doors, finely painted heirlooms, colorful tables, elaborate beds and much more. It was a home decor paradise.

In Jodhpur, we rode horses and camels and explored old fortresses and palaces. But mostly we went shopping. We came back from India with full suitcases and a 40-foot shipping container to follow. It was so much stuff, I had to knock down my fence and cut down two trees to get the container to the house. The truck driver was a guy named Dion from Baltimore and I told him his name meant meditation in Punjabi. He was like, "respect". Then we got to work.

We did demolition and tear outs. We did paint and drywall work. We did road building and deck making. We built a building. We offered blood, sweat and tears to the project. We prayed hard. We got cheated a few times. We battled torrential rains, super-hot days and the frigid cold winds. But mostly we made new friends. We watched the river. We hiked and practiced yoga and sat by the open bonfire. Ten months later, we opened. Soul works like this. When we have so many ways to win, we know we are in touch with soul.

When we meet others full of life, we say "they got soul". Their energy is effervescent. Happy people make other people happy. And hurt people go on to hurt people.

I have done so many dumb things with no soul, too.

When I was in school at the University of Oregon, coffee kiosks selling espresso popped up on every corner in Eugene. On a trip back East, I realized there were no drive thru coffee kiosks. I thought this was a great opportunity. With my step-brother, we formed a company called "Awakenings Coffee" with the intention of becoming a drive thru chain in Virginia. We wrote a business plan. I borrowed money. I got a job as a barista at Starbucks to learn the trade at $8.50 per hour. I was committed.

I learned to make coffee, espresso, caramel macchiatos, frappuccinos, and mochas. I learned about the differences in Indonesian, Costa Rican, and other growing climates for coffee. I cleaned bathrooms and ran the till. I had a good attitude. I wore my green apron with a clean white shirt and tan khakis every day. I got a uniform exception to keep my beard and wear a turban. My manager said I, too, could be a manager one day.

Then it dawned on me. I don't like coffee. And it's not just coffee. It's the concept.

The customers were drug addicts, hooked on caffeine. The pastries were a crime. This wasn't food. There were 40 grams of sugar in those things. It was like injecting diabetes into people. I had changed. I started selling customers on soy and skim milk. I discreetly put in less syrup in the mochas. I pushed the healthiest pastries from the displays. I had a coffee dealer guilt complex. I had no soul. And it wasn't the coffee's fault. It was mine. I cared what people were putting in their bodies. I disregarded my own dharmify step 1. I read *"Pour Your Heart Into It"* by Howard Shultz, CEO of Starbucks at the time. He wrote, "It wasn't until I discovered Starbuck's that I realized what it means when your work truly captures your heart and your imagination." So, for him it was soul, but for me, it was soulless.

A couple of drunks came in one time and asked me the meaning of my name. I explained the story. Hargobind translates as "sustainer of the world". A guy replied, "Then, what the fuck are you doing making coffee?" Prophets come in many forms.

I invested four months in trying to get my first kiosk set up. When my location fell through, I was stuck with a prefabricated building and nowhere to put it. I was now pissed off, broke, and in debt. I didn't respect the soul.

I would fail other times, in epic ways. But there was a difference: I had soul in the work, so it didn't matter. At Casa Om Potomac, I was reflecting on my losses a lot by the river in West Virginia. General Lee from the American Civil War once got trapped along the Potomac nearby. After his Confederate forces lost at the battle of Gettysburg in 1863, he retreated and got stuck at the river while fleeing South. For seven days they waited for the river to recede after losing a vicious battle. I imagine General Lee knew he was going to lose the war as he waited on the Maryland side staring at West Virginia. The less experienced Union General Meade could have finished the Rebels right there on the river by my house. Lee was trapped. He must have known if he couldn't beat the Union at Gettysburg, he would never get a chance to wreak havoc in Union territory again. I wondered how many people in the past got stuck at the Potomac River barrier too. While camped nearby on July 8th 1863 General Lee wrote:

"I shall therefore have to accept battle if the enemy offers it, whether I wish to or not, and as the result is in the hands of the Sovereign Ruler of the universe and known to him only, I deem it prudent to make every arrangement in our power to meet any emergency that may arrive."

In pre-European times, Native Americans wandered up and down what became the main U.S. Highway 81 nearby. They called it "The Great Warrior Trail" which history reminds me of the Grand Trunk Road. Warriors, merchants, and trappers would travel it following the seasons, livestock and opportunity like the other Indians on GT road. It was obviously unpaved, and rugged. Mud ran dangerously deep. Knowing my adversity in this land paled in comparison to those of the past, gave me comfort.

For a bit, it wasn't clear to me where my funding would come from to finish the project. There was a real chance I would lose control of the property in utter defeat. Just as my architect had predicted, and my subcontractors had whispered, I was in trouble. On the one hand, the $350,000 that I owed was not a lot of money given the size of the project. On the other hand, when you owe that kind of money to a variety of strangers all at once, it is incredibly stressful. People get unpredictable, destructive, and sometimes violent when they feel cheated. Screwing people over is never part of my soul. I had to figure it out and like Lee said, my fate "was in the hands of the Sovereign ruler of the Universe".

I had failed before, but this was different because I followed my soul. There was no one to blame but me. That's all I hope for. This way if I lose, I learn. And if I win, it's momentum in a meaningful direction.

This concept of soul comes from Guru Nanak's Japji. Japji is the combination of two words Jap -Recitation and ji - Soul. I think of it like working on your soul. Guru Nanak is the founder of the Sikh religion. His recitation starts the Siri Guru Granth Sahib which is 1430 pages long. And just like Japji is the intro to this longer script, the concept of Ji is the intro to the best version of your longer story. My takeaway from the Sikhs is, always start with the soul. Each action done with soul adds to what I call an upward spiral.

Spirals go both directions unfortunately. I met a guy in jail in Leesburg many years ago. I didn't think my crime was serious, but the judge did. I was driving at 95 miles per hour in a 55 mile an hour zone. In Virginia, they call it "driving with the intent to kill." Punishment calls for two to five days of mandatory jail time. My cell mates got there first so they got the bunks. I slept on the floor like I did back in Punjab. The jail was overcrowded. I was next to the toilet. I am 6'2, so I slept with my feet towards the bowl. That way my face wouldn't get peed on. As time wore on, I noticed the legs of my orange, one-piece jumper got more stinky each time my cellmates relieved themselves.

In dangerous situations I follow the Ben Franklin ethos, who said after signing the Declaration of Independence, "we must all hang together, or, most assuredly, we shall all hang separately". So I got to know my inmates. It reminded me of boarding school. Networking and alliances are the keys to survival. Even if you aren't the strongest, you can work your way to safety by embedding into the crowd.

I quickly realized it was a criminal convention. I met a guy who could convert AR15's to automatic weapons. I met a guy who forged prescriptions for medicinal drugs. I met drug dealers who made their living selling weed, heroin and cocaine. I met a pimp who ran hoes who could smoke cigarettes with their vaginas. I arrived for a speeding ticket and I exited with a network to launch a criminal empire.

These guys are just the context though. It was my broken cellmate that interested me the most. He was in a downward spiral.

He was unsure when he would get out. He didn't know how many times he had been locked up. He had one vice that kept him coming back. Drinking Alcohol. So, he would get out of jail and drink. He would run out of money and get a DUI going to work. His car would break down and then he would lose his job. Stuck at home he would get depressed and then drink more. His fines would pile up. Jobless, he would not be able to pay. So back to jail he would go again. He was lost in the system. He was stuck in a destructive spiral. His soul was lost.

He was a nice guy. I liked him. He gave me a tie for my hair after the cops searched me naked and pulled my turban off. I wish I could have done something for him, but the downward spirals kept him down.

The spirals help us see how we are using momentum to our advantage or how momentum is crushing us.

Ghosts

"Now I know what a ghost is. Unfinished business, that's what."
— Salman Rushdie, Satanic Verses

When I first started looking for soul in the dharmify process, there were many things that came up. I originally reflected on soccer, sports, going back to India, living in Mexico, learning new languages, yoga, spending time with my family and more. As I got deeper, I found there were numerous passions that I thought I had, but which upon further review didn't have much meaning. I call these ghosts.

They hang around sucking a little bit of energy from us, but we never really commit to seeing them through. When I started dharmifying, I started eliminating things as much as I was adding them. If it doesn't show up on your daily dharmify, then it's probably not important. Eliminating what doesn't matter makes time for the things that do. So, I weed things out at the soul stage, leaving in just the things that are super meaningful.

When I dharmify daily, the same few meaningful things keep popping up. Soul should be expressed regularly or it's likely a ghost.

These are three ghosts I had carried with me until I eliminated them:

- Trying to be a soccer star;
- Going back to live in India; and
- Trying to be the best basketball player on the court.

I still love these things. They would be great, but they are no longer in the top category. I let them go making space for other more meaningful things. In fact I was playing soccer 6 nights a week until we opened our first yoga studio. Yoga is a practice that keeps coming up for me in step 1.

A deep connection to the soul has helped me navigate so many yoga scandals.

I took my first class in Bikram yoga with Emmy Cleaves in Los Angeles in the summer of 2001. Siri Om and I suspect we were in that same class together even though we would not meet until 2005.

I liked the hot yoga practice right away but wouldn't start a regular practice until we got together.

In 2010, we went to Bikram Choudhury to ask permission to open a Bikram style hot yoga studio. He was trying, at the time, to build a franchise, but it was highly dysfunctional. His terms were aggressive, unclear, and challenging to follow. They were ultimately so abusive as to be deemed illegal, but they put us in a bind on how to open the business.

Siri Om felt he had already told her she could open as he had all his original students. Unfortunately, she had nothing on paper. We had signed a commercial lease but were struggling to close the deal on what to call the studio. We went to a lecture with Bikram and he boasted of stealing shoes from tourists at a temple in Calcutta. He was a mischief maker, and I felt an affinity for him. He was living the other Indian dream.

The Indian dream, like the American dream, is the same rags to riches story. The other Indian dream was to come to America, make a million dollars and have as much sex as possible.

Listening to Bikram brag, I remembered my shoes were stolen at a temple in India. My friends at the time chided me for being so dumb. Obviously, you never wear your Adidas to the Golden Temple. They would be stolen in a heartbeat. You wear your cheap flip flops called *chappals*.

If it was ok for Bikram to steal my shoes, I concluded, it was ok for me to move ahead with the business. We made the calculation that, if there were a problem, we would negotiate like I used to back in India. We went ahead and opened the Bikram Yoga studio without a licensing agreement in place.

A few years after this, Bikram would lose his copyrighted 26+2 yoga sequence and his franchise concept fell apart. I wasn't surprised by this and we made the right choice to not sign his terms. I had been to Calcutta and practiced yoga in the park with a 90-year-old man who had marched to the sea with Gandhi as a child. He protested the English salt tax during Indian Independence along with most of West Bengal. He told me about the energy of revolution at the time and how it formed him as a boy. Watching the birth of a nation was electric, he said. I could feel his enthusiasm all these years later. He also mentioned they had been doing a standing sequence and floor sequence almost identical to the Bikram poses since he was a child long before Bikram. It wouldn't make sense for someone to come to America and copyright a movement system that was already commonplace in India.

In hindsight, it was a risk worth taking. The yoga studio provided the financial foundation for all the future things we have accomplished. If I hadn't had my shoes stolen in India, we may not have built Bikram Yoga Fairfax.

The Bikram Yoga studios - we grew to own two - provided another unique challenge when Bikram was accused of numerous rapes and sexual assaults. The press was so bad, the business started to tank. We knew there was always lots of sex happening but the evidence emerging was making it clear there were egregious abuses of power. Finally, we had to ask, we love hot yoga, but do we want Bikram's name on the door?

It became more than just a business decision. My wife said at the time, "If I can't send my daughter to Bikram's teacher training, how could I send someone else's?" She had made up her mind. We were rebranding the studios. We kept saying the Emiliano Zapata quote from Mexico: "It is better to die on your feet, than live on your knees". In hindsight, it was an obvious choice. But at the time, it was contentious. We had teachers quit out of fear of losing their Bikram Yoga Teaching Certification. Other studios told our teachers they couldn't also teach with us if they wanted to teach there. Some thought Bikram might sue us, as he had others, for teaching the copyrighted yoga sequence.

It was a unique business challenge. If we disliked yoga, like I did coffee, this would have been the end. But we are yoga people. We have soul in it. This became a pivot.

We rebranded the business as Pure Om Hot Yoga. We turned the studios around. The setback propelled us forward. Later on, we sold them to Yoga Works Inc. They never would have bought two Bikram studios. This gave us the capital to start at Casa Om Potomac, pushing us forward again.

The journey of soul is ultimately about clarifying what matters and then pouring diesel on the fire as we do in West Virginia.

In the soul step, I write out my connection to soul on paper because it gives me the chance to choose what is important and commit to it.

My mother-in-law gave me the book, "Five Love Languages" by Gary Chapman. You know you're in trouble when you get the Love Languages book. So, I read it.

In it, the author talks about how many couples come to a place where they fall out of love. They then call him and ask for help. His advice is always the same. He says at some point, you've got to choose to love each other. When it gets hard, you will have to decide that you want to love the other person. Great relationships don't just happen. They are a choice. You do it for yourself as much as for the other. Mostly, we make bold choices after harsh and painful experiences. Dharmify will help you move before you have to. It will force you to choose what you love or live with the consequences.

I broke my back when I was 16. I had a compression fracture of my L2 vertebrae. I shrunk about a quarter of an inch.

I was laid out for a month in a Delhi hospital. Then, I shifted to a wheelchair for a period thereafter. My hatha yoga practice really started here.

I couldn't touch my toes. I had regular back pain. My first Ashtanga teacher was horrified, telling me, "you are as old as your spine." I started to practice to alleviate my pain. In other words, yoga loved me. I liked it because it gave me something. I put nothing into it though.

My back would hurt and then I would practice. Then I would feel better and not practice. It took many years to realize that if I wanted to go beyond alleviating my pain, I had to man up. If I wanted real strength and mobility, I had to sacrifice being a lazy taker. If I wanted to transform my skeletal system, I had to love it back. I had to choose to love it.

Yoga became a part of my soul when I chose to love it back. If you're struggling to find things that light you up, I would encourage you to start dhamifying for clarity. Then, see where it takes you as you repeat the process each day. You can do that worksheet at dharmify.com/clarity

Fear and shame also hold us back from polishing the soul.

I have an interesting story about this.

In 1998, I would practice *gatka* daily and was in a *nagar kirtan* outside the Golden Temple. Gatka is a style of sword and stick fighting common to North India. Nagar Kirtans are processions of the Sikh holy book, the Siri Guru Granth Sahib followed by kirtan and often displays of Gatka.

The *Jethadar* of the Akal Takht had recently been released from jail for killing a man and partook in the gathering. The Jethadar is like a Sikh version of a bishop.

He saw a group of us playing and wanted to join. He was tall, strong and handsome with a blue turban and thick black beard. His entourage gave him a weapon and he came in to spar with me. As he began shifting his feet and swinging his stick, his pistol flew out from his belt scraping across the chipped concrete. We took a quick break to secure the firearm and then went back at it. I got pumped up seeing the pistol fly.

After watching his fighting style, I leaned in and hit him like I was trained to do. Perhaps even a little harder than I wanted to. The crowd gasped in horror. This was a huge mistake. Worse than painful, it was disrespectful. I didn't understand. I was just fighting. He took it in good humor. The crowd was enraged, seeing a little white man, disrespect the faith. After the match ended, I was embarrassed. People shamed me, making degrading comments and minor threats. I was supposed to let him win but I didn't know. I wanted to jump out of my skin. I tried to hide in the crowd. Never say "no" to a Mexican and never clobber a Jethadar.

Not long after sparring, the Jethadar hosted me and other white Sikhs in his space. I tried to hide in the crowd and hoped he didn't remember me. He was curious about what drew us to the Punjab. Once we had tea and snacks, he started to open up. He talked about jail and what it was like. He said he had to trust in God and Guru. He talked about how small his cell was. He talked about freedom and how sweet it was to be out.

He continued, there was another thing that helped him through - American TV. His favorite show was Baywatch. As he realized what words escaped his mouth, he clarified that he liked "the underwater scenes because he liked the ocean." Nobody likes the underwater scenes in Baywatch. I went back just to rewatch them. As a bunch of adolescent boys snickered, I too tried to contain my laughter. I looked in his face for the first time. I saw in him, that same feeling in me, when I hit him a little too hard.

So, it's in all of us. No matter how far we get. No matter how many titles or how much status we gather, we all have our moments we wish we could take back. However, when we are deeply in touch with soul, we go there less because we are the person we most want to be, doing what we most want to do. Sex, shame and the paths we choose are worth more discussion.

Clients ask me how I found Casa Om Potomac in West Virginia. For a bit I was telling them this was my first time to Martinsburg. But that's not actually true. There was one other time. I did find the property on Zillow. I put in 5 plus beds and 25 plus acres and hit search. I kept the radius to within two hours of Washington DC, my target market.

I then followed all bodies of water going out. I looked at the Chesapeake Bay. The Atlantic Ocean. I looked at Lake Anna and the Shenandoah River. I followed the Potomac River from

East to West. I noticed something. As soon as I crossed the border into West Virginia, land prices dropped by 50%. I could get twice the land with a building for half the price. I can only attribute that to bias against West Virginia. I like fighting bias. We are all the same in my eyes. So, I jumped into the project forgetting that I had been here one other time.

It was a long time ago.

One of my buddies from India came to Virginia to visit. His girlfriend broke up with him and he was down. I had an idea to cheer him up. Before I thought about it, the words left my mouth like the Jethadar's admission of Baywatch.

See there are many fish in the sea!

Let's hit the strip club (hehe).

Before I knew it we were six people deep. I figured the new experience might help him out of the funk. So off to West Virginia we went.

In my family, we don't exactly talk about etiquette for the strip club. In no Sikh Dharma class was this covered. As we rolled into the parking lot, I noticed neon signs and a building with no windows. Then it hit me, "do I take my turban off?"

In fact, the only real thing I knew about strip clubs came from a story about the famous Maharaja Ranjit Singh of the 1800's. He was issued a punishment of 50 lashes for his sexual indiscretions. The internet says it was for marrying a non-Sikh but the way I heard it, it was because he loved strippers.

The origins of the turban date back to ancient Persia or Egypt. They were worn by Prophet Muhammad in the 600's AD and adopted by lots of different sects of Islam, some groups of Christianity, and lots of nobility in India. In my recent trip to Jodhpur, I was intrigued by how much Rajput culture influenced Sikh culture. From the *kirpan,* (a blade that signifies an article of faith), the name Singh which means lion, to the turban styles, long beards and more.

My mother explained the reason we keep long hair with a story of Samson and Delila from the Bible recounted in Judges. Samson is a powerful warrior who derives his power from his long hair. Eventually he divulges his secret to Delila, his consort. Working with his enemies, Delila betrays him and they shave him to steal his power and bring his downfall. My mother told me to keep my hair long and I would stay strong. Keeping a few rituals of commitment has always held meaning for me, and it is one of my favorite reasons to keep long hair.

More recently, the Sikh adoption of the turban around the 1500's AD came to symbolize the commitment to live a pious life. In practice though, especially for men, it's a major indicator as to whether you are living by the faith or not.

For boys raised Sikh, this can and does become a major cause of social anxiety. It's intense in India but especially for those raised in America. More likely than not, it means as a young boy you will get whistled at for going shirtless and having long hair. You will be mistaken for a girl. You will think twice before joining the football team and wearing a helmet or going to the pool. You will think twice before going to the men's room alone. The strippers and I had more in common than you might think.

My particular turban style comes from a specific school in India. Others wear it but especially if you are fair skinned and wear my style, you most likely passed through that school in Amritsar for a period of time.

If you are raised with a turban and make it to age 20, you can assume one of two things. Either A) you own it and it's part of your spiritual path, or B) you've let your community pressure you into something you don't really want to do. You either got soul or you got forced into the group. If you cut your hair, you are to some extent out of the group.

What's a trip about wearing a turban and being white is at any moment you are one hair cut away from blending right back into American society. One of my best friends explained it like this. He said, "When I cut my hair it was like the biggest weight was lifted off my shoulders. I was better looking, more confident and felt like I could do anything."

So, if you have kept your turban for any period of time it means you have dealt with the baggage that comes with it. I spend most of my time in that positive category and I love it. This is what I was processing as we rolled up to the strip club. I wore it to kindergarten. I wore my turban after 9/11. I wore it after the Oak Creek massacre where a white man shot up a

Gurdwara in Wisconsin. I thought, I am going to wear it now. I went into the club with trepidation.

Strip clubs are nice. That was my first thought. The club had granite countertops and great lighting. Everyone looked good in the dim light. My second thought was the women had confidence. They are naked and I am the one afraid. Feeling uncomfortable, I started watching how the money was exchanged. Some guys put dollars into G strings. Others threw it near the pole. Still others used the money to gather attention.

Watching the money, I saw the more confidence a stripper has, the more she would earn. I noticed one particularly beautiful lady that was shy. She was collecting far less than the energetic ones. I drifted to the back and watched.

So even if you were the best-looking stripper, it didn't mean you made the most money. You needed energy. One particularly outgoing stripper hunted me down. She zeroed in and started chatting me up.

My mother always taught me to look a girl in the eye. I probably burned a hole in her face as we covered pole dancing technique. As she went for the kill, she said, "Put the money in your mouth". I did as told and stuck a $5 bill in my new teeth. She then smashed her massive tits into my face and boob-scooped the cash.

The lesson I took away was that when you get super comfortable in your skin, you win. We can all do that in myriad ways, even turbaned up or tits out. We're all thinking, "how do I look" when we should be thinking "how do I make other people feel?"

In Texas Hold 'em poker they say the beginner is playing the cards they are dealt. They think, "What cards do I have to play?" The more advanced player is thinking, "What cards does the other player have?" The still better poker player is thinking, "What does she think I am thinking she's thinking?" Only those who have quieted their anxiety and learned to see outside can have this conversation.

CHAPTER TWO:

KARMA

"The past is never dead. It's not even past."

- William Faulkner

"Old Indian: "Once upon a time, a woman was picking up firewood. She came upon a poisonous snake frozen in the snow. She took the snake home and nursed it back to health. One day the snake bit her on the cheek. As she lay dying, she asked the snake, 'Why have you done this to me?' And the snake answered, 'Look bitch, you knew I was a snake.'"

- Natural Born Killers

The traditional sense of karma is meritorious. You do good, you get good. You do bad, you get bad. This is fine and sometimes true. Still, I prefer a different definition.

My reflection on karma is that our past is massively co-creating our future. It is our primary source of wisdom. Especially if we look at how much our past is repeating itself. When we deeply understand our history, we can be the fortune tellers of our own lives. We can start to look into karma and use it to co-create our future while accounting for the chaos factor.

A potential client called me one time. She said, "I would like to be a vendor at the One Fire hot yoga festival." I said "Great! For $500 you get a table and chairs and a place to display your banner." I asked her what type of service she provides. She said, "I am a fortune teller." I thought that would be so fun as I imagined her giving readings to the participants. We chatted a while about the spirit and intention of the event. She asked, finally, "How many people are coming?" I replied, "Do I sound like a fortune teller to you?"

But just like a great fortune teller, seeing karma provides a map to understanding ourselves. To look into our past gives us great insight into our futures. It clarifies what to do now.

George Santayana once said, "Those who cannot remember the past are condemned to repeat it." Perhaps the more cynical observation is, "What we learn from history is that we do not learn from history." I look into my past with the hopes that I can break my cycles. Mistakes are painful, but repeating mistakes is even more vicious.

Here's how I do karma.

I divide my karma into two categories: success and trauma.

I think of people as if they are carrying around two invisible duffle bags. The first is filled with the things they have accomplished. The schools they have been to. The confidence they have gained. The support from their friends they have earned. The love from their parents they received. The hard knocks that life has given them. This forms their positive views of themselves and the world. It's a comfortable bag of successful karma to explore.

Then there is the trauma.

In the trauma bag we have the abuse. The imposter syndrome. The guilt. The damage. The abandonment. The sexual assaults. The injuries. The broken hearts. The wounds that have never been diagnosed or healed.

In the Yoga Sutras, Patanjali writes that karma, the cycles of action and reaction, are eternal. They are constantly reproducing. So, these traumas are the seeds of the next traumas for us and others. Therefore, we have to heal. Because, otherwise, the hurt and pain inflicted upon us grow into the hurt and pain we inflict upon others.

Just like a great story filled with suspense, our successes and our traumas are in constant fluctuation. They both are reproducing. It's a question of which experiences, with limited resources, are going to reproduce faster and more fruitfully. We cannot fully know until we look directly at and peruse thoroughly the library of our history. **My argument is: the more you understand your past, the more advantage you have on the future.**

The karma of the past is co-creating the future with our current self. We are looking at karma for insight into how we might craft our future. We don't get to control it. Dharmifying is recognizing that we do get to influence it. When these answers are good, we are good. When they are off, we have challenges. Here is where dharmifying helps. We can address our karma with intentional dharma.

As I mentioned earlier, when I was 16, I broke my back jumping off a high building. Back then, there was no parkour, so they just called it stupid. I thought I could land a certain way and I couldn't. I believed in myself. I overcame my fear. Two other jumpers went ahead of me. They landed in a four-point stance and rolled. They landed the right way because they were trained better. They had good karma. I didn't and suffered a compression fracture of my L2 vertebrae.

There were no ambulances in Anandpur Sahib, India at the time. They transported me on the floor of an old bus to Chandigarh some 80 kilometers away for an MRI. As we bumped along down the road, I had a lot of time to think. I was creating karma. I was doing things that would determine future opportunities and struggle. When we don't have enough karma in a space to succeed, the karma creates trauma. This was the one of many times I realized that I shouldn't take such big risks without such big skills.

For a while, I put this experience in my trauma duffle bag. I was in pain. My body didn't move well. I couldn't lean forward at all. Still, karma is a pendulum. Our trauma can become our tools. Sometimes the pendulum swings. Breaking my back is the only kundalini experience I could claim. When I jumped, I landed on my tailbone which took the impact. In kundalini myth, there are seven or eight chakras, or energy centers, residing along the spine. Each chakra holds a special energy. A base of energy resides at the root chakra, down by the coccyx right where I landed. The kundalini starts there and rises like a snake, tapping each energy center along the way, leading to more and more positive growth. The energy spirals upwards, to the brain and eventually out through the aura. This is an energetic path of enlightenment from which I borrowed my upward spiral concept. Physiologically, the impact broke the L2 and caused extreme sensation all the way up my spinal cord and through my brain. Kundalini-wise, it's hard to say what happened, but it was intense.

If this "trauma" hadn't happened, I wouldn't have committed to my health at such an early age. I would not have committed to the yoga practice. I would not have lost the ability to walk. I would not have appreciated walking. I would not have actively tried to leverage my traumas so early on. In these ways, I am so blessed and that's in line with my perception of what should happen in a kundalini awakening.

Likely as I age, and my back-scar tissue factors back into my daily life, the karma pendulum will swing again. Maybe I will feel less blessed.

When most people think of karma, they think of it in a personal sense. I find it also insightful to recognize the influence of family, community, and the nation state in determining our karma.

I will tell you about my family for some context of my karma in the hope that it sparks something insightful in you.

My father's side of the family were Russian Jews who migrated to the United States in the early 1900's. He was raised in Long Island, New York and the phrase my grandmother used to tell him was, "You're a *mensch*. You are going to be a doctor. Until then, take out the trash."

My mother was Irish Catholic. Her grandparents migrated from Ireland around the same time. My Nana (as we called her) had eight kids, seven of whom were boys. She prayed to Mother Mary for a girl and promised to name her Mary. After six boys, my mother Mary arrived. She was the answer to many prayers. As a boy, I would take my Nana to Catholic Church and was so proud to walk her through the pews as she got more and more frail. Things were pretty normal amongst my ancestors of middle class Jewish and Catholic Northeastern American families. And then things went a different direction.

My dad got into medical school but was deeply unhappy. It was the 1960's in America at a time of massive upheaval. He found kundalini yoga, the teachings of Yogi Bhajan, and decided to change his life drastically. He went home and declared to his adoring Jewish parents: change was coming. He had taken traditional Sikh vows known as Amrit Sanchar. Clad in a white turban, a traditional Sikh kurta and short beard, he told them he legally changed his name to Sat Want Singh Khalsa. He announced he dropped out of medical school to become a dishwasher in a vegetarian restaurant. He had joined an ashram. In West Virginia, we describe an ashram as a trailer park for yogis. Other people just called it a cult. And he was now a Sikh, a vegetarian and would give up shaving, alcohol, and drugs.

The story they tell about my mother is no less bold. The guy she brought home to my grandparents first was a black man. At the University of Massachusetts, she met him through her volunteer work with the Black Panther Party. She believed in racial equality and worked to instill that value in me. My grandparents, coming from thousands of years of Irish Catholic ancestry likely envisioned something different for her. I am told they were respectful of her choices. That relationship ended for reasons unknown to me. Then, at some point, she also went home dressed in all white, wearing a turban, and declared she was no longer Mary Mullin, the answer to Nana's prayers. She took Sikh vows and legally changed her name to Sat Nam Kaur Khalsa.

The way I read it, when that didn't shock them enough, she returned home with my dad.

They met at the ashram in Washington DC where they worked in one of the city's first vegetarian restaurants called the Golden Temple Conscious Cookery.

When my parents were married in a traditional Sikh wedding, the Jews and Catholics arrived not knowing that their heads needed to be covered in a Gurdwara. So, my Uncle Joe who lived nearby, ran home and returned with his hat collection. He brought top hats, baseball caps, fedoras, and panama hats. Then there were yarmulkes and turbans too.

My two grandmothers met before the wedding and cried incessantly. They went out that night and got super drunk to numb the pain related to what their children had done. And that's how I got here. You could say I am the product of a rich, diverse cultural heritage, or a total fucking mess.

When I left for India, I felt so much relief from the pressure of American society. Between school, financial trouble, wearing a turban, Sikhism, keeping long hair, puberty, the suburban lifestyle, and the pressure from my parents, the community was crushing me. India was a blessing. As I grew into a different person, my friends from boarding school became my crew. I loved it so much. Then I graduated and I was alone once again. This happened a few times until I realized the community is karma that we can develop. When I listen to military veterans or athletes from team sports, they often deal with this type of communal karma as well.

In the karma stage, we ask: is the family we have and the community we are from working for us? In turn, are we being fair to them? If the answer to either of these is no, major parts of your future are already determined with struggle and conflict. If you are not being cared for from your family and community, then your ability to create is limited. Alternatively, if you are not caring for family and community, then they will come and punish you eventually. By studying your karma, you can leverage your karma.

The karma of the nation state we are from is also influencing us in drastic ways. I have always been grateful for my American heritage, even when I felt so much rejection there. I love the basic American values of individualism, equality, liberty, and the pursuit of happiness. I love the Constitution and that document influenced my approach to dharma. I think some of the criticism is valid as well. The nuances of a country's history is the best example of a karmic pendulum.

I think we made the single greatest blunder of the 21st century, so far, with the invasion of Iraq. The death, carnage, and destruction that we unleashed on that tiny country for no reason is indefensible, arrogant and ultimately futile.

It was the main reason I went on a tsunami relief mission to the Andaman Islands in 2004. My logic went like this. Three thousand Americans died in the attacks on 9/11. Now we are amassing 250,000 soldiers to unleash hell on a place that had nothing to do with it, produced no terrorists, rejected wahabist jihadist ideology at the time, and was too weak to pose a threat to the region. If anything, Iraq was a bulwark to the complex competing interests of Iran. Around the same time, a massive tsunami killed 200,000 people across Indonesia, India, and South Asia. I thought, maybe instead, we should do something worthwhile about that.

If 250,000 Americans are ready to deploy for the wrong fight, the least I could do was to be part of a different American story. So, I signed up with a group called United Sikhs and travelled with a small team of Americans to Chennai, India to play a support role in a tsunami relief trip. Our mission had 4 objectives. Deliver supplies and cash. Help document losses of the locals. Generate publicity and assist in rebuilding homes.

The only problem was I had no karma here. I had no basic skills. However, I also knew that I didn't want to be defined as going to the wrong fight or, worse, an American that complains and does nothing. If I could develop some karma in relief work, maybe in the future I would have something to contribute to humanity.

On the mission, we immediately ran into problems. The Andaman Islands are contested territory. The Indians, Chinese and others claim it as their own. Campbell Bay was our intended destination where a small community lost a lot of people and industry. But foreigners are not supposed to go there because of a military base nearby. We had to get special permission from the Governor of Tamil Nadu who claims jurisdiction over the islands. So, off to the governor's mansion we went.

The mansion was an old palace left from the British occupation. In it was a tall imposing Sikh, named Surjit Singh Barnala, which normally would be unusual for South India. He was once a dominant force in Punjab politics rising to Chief Minister. He almost made it as far as Prime Minister of India before his rivals pounced. The way I read it, they stuck him in a Tamil Nadu honey pot so he would get out of the way of the next generation of Punjab leaders. And a honey pot he got. His mansion was epic. He was well versed in the history of the White Sikhs having attended a few of their summer solstice celebrations in New Mexico. He even became a vegetarian after a meeting with some of them in the 1970's. He gave me his book and wished us well on the relief mission. He gave us special permission to enter Campbell bay. I think it was partly because I was an American Sikh. I thanked him greatly and headed for the sea.

I slept on the deck of a boat for three days as we traversed the Indian Ocean. I saw the most epic sunsets and ate the weirdest yellow dahl below deck. After three days we arrived and did the best we could. We spent time documenting losses for people that spoke no English. We delivered a bunch of cash and goods we raised. We planned a sports day for the kids with prizes. It became a whole celebration and the whole island attended.

We realized the majority of people that died actually drowned in waist high water. They couldn't swim. So, the majority of death occurred amid panic. We spent some time teaching kids to swim and finding their footing in the ocean. It was simple but the small stuff actually had the most impact. If anything, we brought some hope. That was the most memorable contribution. The massive destruction was more than a few kids could change. The mission had mixed results, but we showed up. We tried and I learned.

Personally, I was happy to be the type of American I was. I generally stick close to this ideology. If I am not happy with my country karma, I ask what exactly I have done about it. That has kept me in a positive view of where I am from. Resolving this karma is a source of major healing for each of us. If you dislike your country, I recommend you dharmify it.

Your family, the community, and the pack, are very much part of your karma. They are important factors in stating what you can and cannot do. They are the foundation of your past and they are propelling you into the future. Finding the overlap of soul and karma creates dharma. This is the transition from our past to the future. They meet at the present moment illuminating the path we are on.

One of my basic business philosophies comes from this view of karma. Take what they do well in one village and bring it to another that doesn't yet have it.

Deeply understanding the karma and soul questions will clarify the most conscious path to creating your future. This comes together in dharma.

CHAPTER THREE:
DHARMA

"I have been sent to this world by the Lord to propagate dharma"

Guru Gobind Singh

noun: the eternal and inherent nature of reality, regarded in Hinduism as a cosmic law underlying right behavior and social order.

Plan or be planned upon.

- My uncle, United States General John Mullin

Everyone has a plan until they get punched in the mouth

- Mike Tyson

Somewhere on the backstreets of Buenos Aires, I made a nice connection with my taxi driver. He told me of his military service. He showed me the scar from a bullet on his forehead. We bonded over our mutual distaste of English imperialism. He nearly died in the Falkland wars. He is lucky he survived as many of his friends perished.

I was traveling with two heavy bags and my flight wasn't for another 14 hours. My new friend, or so I thought, offered to hang on to my stuff for the day while I took in the cultural sights of the city. He knew I may never return. Trust a stranger with all my stuff and then look the fool I thought.

I paused for a minute. I realized I would trade what I had, for a good day in Buenos Aires. So I took him up on the offer. I went exploring little European inspired cafes and the opera house. I went to the zoo and watched the animals. I dreamed of what life would be like at the South end of the world.

Fourteen hours passed. I stood exactly where he told me to meet him.

He showed up with the integrity of a soldier just as I thought he would. I smiled in recognition of how good people can be. I took my bags. Hugged my friend. Then boarded my plane and said goodbye to the beautiful country. The con never arrived.

I was thinking about this many years later in Mexico City. I boarded a taxi once again with heavy bags. Always chatty, I made a new friend. We spoke of Casa Del Tono and the great food of Distrito Federal. I was rushing to make it on tour with Snatam Kaur to sell CD's. The driver took me to the Paraguay embassy, the Brazilian embassy and then for a quick stop at the juice bar. Diligently waiting on me at each stop. Only this time, I left my computer bag in the taxi. As I stepped out of the car for a quick second, he sped away with all of my possessions.

I stood on the side of a busy highway waiting, hoping it was all a mistake. Mexico felt so warm until it didn't. The con finally arrived. It just came 12 years later and thousands of miles from Argentina.

After what seemed an eternity of watching traffic, I remembered that I would take a day of freedom in Buenos Aires even if I had to drop baggage in Mexico City. Trusting a stranger was still the right choice.

Wikipedia states, "In Hinduism, dharma signifies behaviors in accord with Rta, the order that makes life and universe possible, and includes duties, rights, laws, conduct, virtues and the "right way of living."

My concept of dharma is inspired from the Indian religions. While I have more liberal tendencies, my thinking is also influenced by the conservative American philosopher Leo Strauss.

He argued that the problem with liberal thinking is it fails to arrive at a conclusion that this is the best way forward. I fundamentally believe there is a best way and it's found by looking at soul and karma. For simplicity sake, my definition of dharma is **the right choice**. The dharmify process leads there. So, there is a best choice, but it's unique to each of us. The usefulness of dharma in this context is that doing this process will reveal to you your best choice, which may or may not align with a belief system.

Where soul and karma overlap, we create dharma. Mostly we are unconscious about this. We simply have desires and a past that have brought us here. When we align soul and karma and consciously choose a dharma, we maximize our focus on what's most meaningful.

Soul + Karma = Dharma

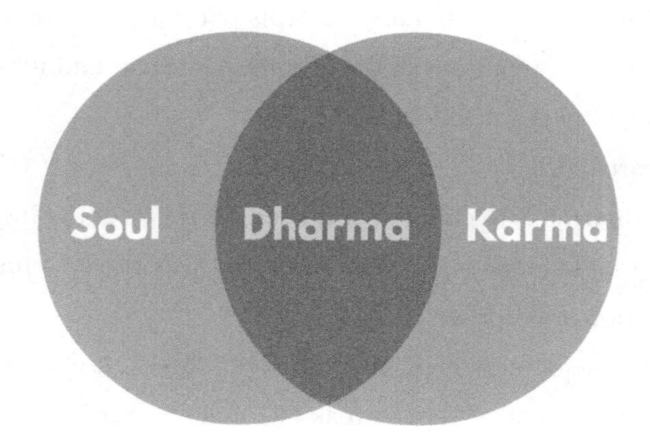

None of this is new. But the process revealed to me that I was sadly, constantly jumping to dharma without taking soul along for the leap (Awakenings Coffee); or wondering why I was failing when I had no karma in the space (Casa Om Mexico and Potomac construction).

At this stage, I can reflect on the ghosts that I am carrying with me. These ghosts are the things that I am holding onto, but I don't have the energy to pursue. They haunt me. They take my energy. They create self-defeating thoughts about my lack of success. This is the time to drop them. Kill the ghosts.

So, it is from this fusion of my soul and karma, I crafted this dharma 3 years ago for the year.

My dharma is to be a yoga master and uplift people through revolutionary yoga studios, hotels, festivals, and training.

We were in the midst of rebranding our Bikram Yoga studios and building the Casa Om Retreat Center concept. So, this idea of building revolutionary concepts with major growth was paramount. I wanted out of the Bikram paradigm and into my own thing. But it got so busy.

In early 2020:

My dharma is to chill out and keep what I've got going.

I worked almost a full year straight. I was tired. I finished construction at Potomac.

Then the pandemic hit, and I got a nice break. It was a great pause for me. I hadn't had a break like that since 2004.

Then, in mid-2020, my dharma became:

My dharma is to finish the dharmify book, become a master of internet marketing and invest time into being a better family man.

Why did it change? Because my soul and karma changed.

Do this process again and again and you will see how much you change. Being aware of that gives you so much insight.

As I started doing dharmify daily, the dharmas got way more simple like:

Focus on things that mean something

Be a highly functioning human with many things in alignment

Be two steps ahead of everyone's needs.

Be a great papa, advance my book, get ready for the group and work out

In addition to the above, there are two more benefits of dharma:

First, it becomes easy to say "no." Many years ago, pre-dharmify, I was pitched with the idea of taking over a motorcycle supply ecommerce site by one of my best friends. I have skills in ecommerce and website development. I had some karma here. The price was right, and the market was big. I spent 3 days reviewing the concept. I was taken by the opportunity to do something new. However, as I went deeper, it was another Awakenings Coffee.

I don't like wearing a helmet. It doesn't fit over my turban. I have no tattoos. I don't drink. I don't like bars. My wife would kill me if I brought home a motorcycle. In short, I would be the most imposter biker ever. I have no soul here. I spent 72 hours thinking about this. I could have just reviewed my dharma and turned it down immediately. I wasted 3 days. Every business idea should get dharmified.

If it doesn't fit my dharma, I just say "no." Sometimes I even show people my dharma, so they don't take it personally. It's extra helpful when turning down all my friends selling me Do-Terra.

The second additional benefit of finding clear dharma is it will make you feel very good about your choices. Buddha says, "It is better to travel well, than to arrive." Factors out of our control can create a real negative story around us. As you start to dharmify daily, it will give you small actions to take that will build a positive story around what you control.

When your dharma is clear, then when you lose you are gaining experience and knowledge in meaningful spaces. Every loss becomes an increase in usable karma which you'll likely use because it's attached to soul.

Never was this step more important than when we rebranded the Bikram studios. If our stated goal was to be the greatest Bikram yoga studio, we would have a tremendous problem. Things out of our control were at play. The value of the brand plummeted. We were all of a sudden in the wrong business.

Because our purpose was simply to share yoga, we could pivot. We were not attached to the brand-specific outcome.

Dharmify can be used to create the why for goal setting. I am a huge fan of goal setting but it's not always situationally appropriate. After you dharmify, set the goals. Then you can dharmify to reach the goals each day. There are no goals in dharmify unless you want them. The only universal reason to do this is to find contentment.

The difference between goals and dharma became clear in building Casa Om Mexico. At one point, my goal was to build a 100-room hotel that I could use as a festival and retreat center in the United States. As I began pricing it out, the economics were impossible. I knew it would work. I knew everyone would win but I simply didn't know anyone who would back a $10,000,000 project.

I felt like I was failing. Nothing was happening. But it was silly. So much was going well for me. I started to dig deeper. I asked myself what about my soul and karma is drawing me this direction. Forget the goal. How could I start with the resources I had?

Pretty soon the idea morphed into Casa Om Mexico. It's 12 bedrooms. I can share my love for hospitality with the guests. I can make them delicious food. I can share yoga practice with them. We can do smaller events and plan festivals on the beach. It allows me to pursue everything I care about but on a distinctly smaller scale. Let's be real though. If we are goal setting, then

I am failing. But I am 100% on point with my dharma. That's why I recommend this approach because sometimes the win is to stop goal setting and appreciate what we got.

Once I reach a dharma, I also often go backwards if I don't like it. If I am dharmifying an idea, I often come to the conclusion that I don't have enough karma here to go forward, so I pivot.

For a period, every time I went to the airport, my suitcases would be overweight. I was that guy always shifting stuff around to get under 50 pounds while everyone stared at the contents of my suitcase. I had the idea that a self-weighing suitcase would be a "great idea." I started working on designs and drawing it out. Eventually I found that I didn't have the manufacturing karma. I didn't have the connections to make it. I didn't have enough soul in the idea to see it forward. Mostly, I was just mad at my wife for overpacking. So, there was no dharma. I skipped it and moved on to the next thing without wasting much energy. It wasn't my path. People later built this and made lots of money. It was their path.

Another note about crafting your dharmas. They should be easy to sense when you are faking it or crossing your own integrity. If your dharma is to live sober, say it clearly so you know when you are crossing yourself.

I took a class on U.S. constitutional law from Matt Manweller at the University of Oregon. I remember his argument clearly. The U.S. constitution is the longest serving legal document guiding a country in the world.

The framers wrote it with two intentions. First, lawyers and judges had a guide to make clear decisions. And second, it contained processes for adjustments with the times. You can edit and redo these all the time. As Archibald Cox would say, the dharmas have room for judicial review. Great dharma statements work in this way so that you can clearly say, "yes I am following my dharma" or "no, I have crossed my own self." Each time you do the process you can do your own judicial review.

If we like our dharma, then we continue forward. If we don't like them, then we go back to soul and karma and look for better stuff.

Great dharmas are summaries of complex stories. With our thoughts, we are telling ourselves things all day, every day. We have a soundtrack playing constantly. The dharma statement is the chance to influence the internal dialogue. I use dharma as a mantra. Sometimes I also distill it down to a single word.

Many of the traditions of India use the concept of mantra. In sanskrit "man" comes from the word *manas*: which means mind. "Tra" means action. So, you are taking action on the mind through your recitation of the words you use. Through the recitation of prayers, the names of God or sounds, devotees of the practice found they could reach states of enlightenment.

My idea here comes from Patanjali's ancient argument on the goal of yoga. Patanjali wrote an original self-help book, Yoga Sutras of Patanjali, around 1500 BC. In this book, he presents the limbs of yoga with 8 steps for self-work including yoga poses, deep breathing, right action, avoidance of wrong action, meditation, concentration, sense withdrawal, and *samadhi,* which I still don't understand. He then suggests that you can do all that work or take the easy route. Alternatively, you can just practice *ishvara pranidhana,* known as devotion to God through the recitation of mantra. His argument is that a) you can work really hard or b) chant the mantra and get your head right.

There is a story of Kabir in India. He was a poet and spiritual figure in the 1400's AD. Kabir was born Muslim but he wanted to study with the Guru, Ramanand. Ramanand was Hindu and wouldn't accept Kabir. So Kabir noticed Ramanand would recite his mantras every morning on the way to taking a cold bath in the river. So Kabir got an old blanket and hid on the path to the river. Ramanand tripped over Kabir one early morning shouting out his mantra "Ram" in surprise. Ram is the name of a Hindu God. This is how Kabir got his mantra.

Kabir became a weaver. He would make baskets and clothes and other things. As he worked, he recited his mantra day and night, "Ram Ram Ram". After many years, the God Ram got fed up. Hearing his name called hour after hour, day after day, year after year, he finally went to visit Kabir. Ram appeared one day and asked Kabir, "what is it that you want?" Kabir said "nothing." So, Ram decided he would follow Kabir and chant "Kabir Kabir Kabir". This is how Kabir found God.

This is how we use dharma. Use it as a mantra. When we train our minds, we first put in the work. Even to get the right mantras, like Kabir did, we must put in the work. Then the recitation begins. Moment after moment spent dharmifying, focusing on what matters most. Then eventually, Ram chases us.

With the Casa Om Potomac project, mantra became my main tool. I made so many mistakes in the construction. It was clear I screwed up the budget. I also screwed up the construction sequence. I didn't realize I would need to put in a commercial sprinkler and fire alarm to convert the building from residential to commercial until the project already started. This required tearing out huge amounts of drywall. It slowed down our painting and caused damage to the work we had already started. It also delayed the project by months stretching my loans and mortgage requirements. These are big mistakes in construction.

I knew I didn't have the money to finish the project. I was feeling inadequate, and straight up dumb. And to make it worse my construction teams knew it. My architect said, "You're not a general contractor." My general contractor before I let him go said, "This is like a mix between the movies the Money Pit and The Shining." My buddy, the tile guy said, "You're in over your head." My carpenter said to his dad "If we mess it up, Hargobind will just pay us to do it again." The way he said it, I knew it wasn't the first time they had that conversation.

When your team knows you are weak, it is very challenging to lead. All I had was my thoughts so I worked on my mindset.

Sometimes I would go to my truck, close the doors, and scream at the top of my lungs, "I CAN FUCKING DO THIS!" I have a video of this and I look totally crazy. I couldn't post it online because, without the context, I just look deranged. My family was already gone. I was broke. No one was coming to save me. Mindset was all I had.

I moved into the property like an occupier. I put a mattress on the floor. Water and power were cut to the house when I first arrived. It was cold. I flushed the toilet with a bucket of water from the broken pool, like I learned to do in India. There was a giant black snake living in the library and I tossed him outside. Like the 7 year old boy getting kicked out of the men's room, I resolved to never leave until it was done. Ever. I had $1,250,000 in life insurance and there was no suicide clause in it. No matter how I died, I was getting paid and the project was getting done. In my mind, I already won.

From mid-May through January, I took about one day off to be with my daughter. There was so much construction debris, I would wrap my bed in a tarp, so it wasn't dusty when I went to sleep. I would start in quiet meditation each morning and then start repeating to myself, "I can do this." Like Kabir reciting Ram, Ram Ram. Each time I felt scared or insecure or criticized, I would listen and learn. In my mind I would repeat "I can do this." Because the criticism around me was true. I had messed up. But there was only one way out. Keep going.

CHAPTER FOUR: VISION

May we see the faults of others and unsee them.

- Ardas, a Sikh prayer

The only thing worse than being blind is having sight but no vision.

- Helen Keller

In the yoga practice, drishti, or vision, is that upon which the eyes are set. It is an important component of the pose. In Ashtanga yoga, a teacher went so far as to tell me without vision there is no pose. It indicates where we are going. By defining a dharma, you trigger a vision. It is either seeing with more consciousness the path you are on, that you affirm your soul and karma; or it is a declaration of a new path forward.

Vision nudges the next step forward. It's both a time to express where we think we are going and where we want to go. Both are helpful. Visionaries are taking the small amount of power they have and controlling what they can control.

When we were building Casa Om in Mexico, I also ran out of money but not nearly as drastically. It was mid-October and we had retreats booked for the end of December. I had 15 people working for me. As I looked into the near future, I knew there was no way we would be ready for the first group. I predicted if we doubled the size of the construction team, we could be ready. Sensing I would miss my deadline, I doubled the team with doubts about my ability to pay. I was out of integrity if I didn't pay my workers; but I was also out of integrity if I didn't deliver for my clients. I needed to clarify what mattered most.

Donald Rumsfeld once described leadership like this. I will summarize because I can't find the exact quote. He said, at the pinnacle of power, when you are leading a country at the top, all decisions are bad decisions. You are always presented with a series of extremely bad options. And why is that? Because if they were easy choices, they would be made somewhere further down the chain of command. So, leaders are branded with their inevitably bad choices because they are all bad choices while the followers are protected from ever having to choose. Obviously, my choice paled in comparison, but it was still a decision on bad options with potentially bad consequences either way I went. Before I judge leadership, I often hold my tongue knowing I have the luxury to not choose because I have the luxury of never having to raise that high. Rumsfeld also said, "the world is run by those who show up".

Around this time, I took my plumber, his cousin and one of my concrete workers on a material run in Cancun. We were buying copper piping and plumbing fixtures for the bathrooms. As we passed a building project on the way back from Home Depot, the plumber pointed to a housing complex. He said his boss there ran out of money on the project and struggled to pay his workers. They came in to work one day and he was dead on the jobsite surrounded by a pool of his own blood. Someone murdered him right there for all to see. The guys all laughed as they looked at me. They knew I was getting tight. I shifted positions uncomfortably in my seat. I understood how winding up dead can happen.

They warned me to never run out of money in Mexico. On the one hand it was dangerous to owe my workers and not pay. On the other hand, I would give everything for my clients and the people that trust me.

I know what happens when the venues aren't what they are promised to be. In India at an event I worked, I learned the hard way. I was in customer service for the 11.11.11 Kundalini Yoga and Music Festival in Rishikesh. The festival was built around the idea that this date and time was to bring a big change in consciousness on the planet. This was the start of a new astrological cycle known as the Aquarian Age.

The venue was an ashram and ashrams are generally run down and sparse. You go to an ashram to give up stuff. Also, when you have an all-volunteer work force, it's challenging to keep a place at a high standard. We had 400 people come from all over the world. Most of them had never been to India and hated their rooms. The ashram had a guru, and someone accidentally posted a picture of his room on the site so everyone thought they were getting something way better than they were. His room was decorated with beautiful hand carved furniture from Jodhpur. Later on, we got our Casa Om Potomac furniture from this same vendor.

At the festival, I was put in charge of everyone who hated their rooms. It was 5 couples who were all commiserating together. They had flown for 18 plus hours, travelled by bus even further, and were now tired, culture-shocked, hungry and distraught about their living spaces.

I came up with a strategy. I recruited a customer service team and assigned someone to each enraged couple, and we spaced them out. If we could keep them from complaining with each other, it would slow the momentum. It would diffuse a downward spiral. Plus, I knew everyone had flown for hours and if I walked them around long enough, eventually they would settle into their rooms out of exhaustion. I had no other choice. I had to get these people in their rooms. I decided to take the most pissed off Australian couple and wear them out. I showed them another room and it was horrible. There was no toilet, just an open pit, like my old jail cell. There was no natural light and no view. The mattress felt like cardboard stuffed in a bed sheet. The floor was dusty and unfinished like the setting of a horror movie.

I noticed the Australian guy's massive hands as if they wanted to form in a fist. I kept the threat walking in front of me as it crossed my mind, he might punch me. Brawling in the streets of Rishikesh was not how I envisioned the dawning of the Age of Aquarius.

Finally, the guy looked to me and said, "You know what, fuck kundalini yoga, fuck yogi bhajan and fuck you! We are leaving on the next flight to Australia" I felt terrible, assumed a firm stance and said, "I have 1 more room to show you". It also sucked but by the time we got there, they just wanted to go to sleep.

The event was epic. The main hall was situated right by the Ganges River with sweeping water views and sunsets. We sat where yogi's sat for thousands of years. The monkeys were hilarious. They would rip holes in the tent and stick their heads in while we practiced yoga. A 104-year-old sadhu explained his secrets of longevity. The swamis and kirtan wallahs were fascinating. And Gurmukh who led the event taught epic classes. She made the room situation just another obstacle on the path. The whole experience was a once in a lifetime chance to be part of a special event. Four days later, the Australian was dressed like a sadhu with an orange bindi on his forehead. He looked like he changed from a villian in the Street Fighter video game to a hippy from the Beatles. He came up and gave me an apology and a massive hug. I apologized too and I was so grateful that he stayed.

Still, I swore I wouldn't be that guy messing up the venue and disappointing the clients in Mexico. I had already learned that lesson.

So, I figured if I pursued the idea that we were opening on time and the way we promised, I just needed to come up with more money to pay my workers. There was really only one option and it was to go all in. I outlasted the Australian in India; I would outlast my workers in Mexico.

We did two things. First, we ran the most aggressive discounted daily deals ever for our Bikram yoga studio in Fairfax, Virginia. In hindsight this was an epic decision. We made so much money in so little time. If we weren't under such financial pressure from building, we never would have gone so aggressively to make money.

General business theory says that, in a commodifying market, the company that drops prices first and deepest, claims the lion share of the revenue. The market was commodifying because there were so many yoga studios opening. We had our best year ever at the yoga studio while we were building Casa Om. I was in Mexico almost the whole time. It also gave lots of people exposure to yoga at rock bottom prices. So that was a karma win for me. I still have people that thank me for introducing them to yoga at this time.

We did deals like 20 classes for $20 and sold 2500 passes. We did annuals for $599 and sold 242 passes. I remember getting an ACH deposit for $116,000. I talked the discount deal companies into an 80-20 split. I said they would never get a deal like this. They would never meet a yoga entrepreneur like me. Yogi Bhajan once told me to become a yoga teacher and a businessman and I would make half a million dollars without moving my pinky just like him. So I inked the deals on docusign with just my pinky moving as little as possible. We had a $250,000 month with costs of $30,000. Our vendor rep said all of the senior people were using us as a model to pitch other studios on how to run deals.

Some yoga studio owners looked down on me for this. They would say things like Groupon ruined yoga. That to me was always crazy. In my view yoga was always meant to be free. I have always tried to share what I know regardless of price. I was just charging because that was the economic system in which we all live. Our accountant asked how we could be making that much money with such a phenomenal margin. He asked if we were money laundering, but it was 100% legitimate yoga. I told him the other option was getting murdered by my workers in Mexico. I had the right motivation.

This is really the vision. To see the problems ahead of time. So that we can make our best possible choices. For me, pain that is coming my way is not so bad if I know it's coming.

Seeing ahead is a step ahead.

Ideas are dharma. Vision is our best case scenario of what happens next. Like the cliché, a butterfly flaps its wing in Hawaii and causes a tsunami in Japan. Small movements reverberate over time. At one of my festivals, someone complimented me, "It's like we are walking in the mind of Hargobind". The more we live in the positive creation of our own mind, the greater the satisfaction becomes.

This is how dharma and vision relate. Our ability to perceive the future allows us to ask the question "do I really want to take this path?" Once you have declared a dharma, there is a repercussion, and using vision, you guide yourself.

In Sat Nam Rasayan, a meditative healing, one of the core teachings is "All I know is what I feel."

I use this extensively in vision. When I imagine the future and ask, "how do I feel having spent 5 years doing this thing?", or in dharmify daily, "how do I feel tonight if this is my dharma today"? My feelings become so truthful. If I don't like how I feel, I go back and modify dharma.

This is an important part of the process because vision cultivates the seeds we are planting with our dharma. In yoga practice we call them *bija* mantras or seed mantras. Seeing where those intentions are taking you is an important compass on where you are going.

In my workshops, when we start working with vision, there can be this awkward pressure that infiltrates the group. There can be an implication that we must want to do something. It's not true! Don't fall in that trap. The key question is are you content? If you are not, then do something.

Vision helps us to stop pretending we are happy when we are deeply unsatisfied. When we reach the deep level of dissatisfaction, we go back to dharma. We look again at soul and karma. Tie in the things that have the most charge to dharma and your visions will be clear, fun and powerful.

When I was a little boy, my mother used to tell me a bedtime story about our neighbor's cat. It became a mythical cat named Raja that would go on adventures through the neighborhood. She would go to 7-11. She would go to the park. She would sneak in the neighbors houses and drink milk. When my daughter was born, I too needed some mythical heroes to share with her before bed. I resurrected Raja.

In our stories Raja began leading Siana all over the world. Raja took her to India to study with the Himalayan masters. Raja took her to China to learn about the history of the Mongols and the Great Wall. Raja went to Wall street to be a corporate titan. Raja took her to Antarctica to learn about climate change. Finally, she went to Egypt to see the pyramids and learn about a society in flux.

At the end of the journey, we returned home to settle into bed. At the conclusion of the trip, Siana asked me, "But papa, I have one question. What was I wearing?" I told her a Cinderella dress. She expressed her satisfaction and drifted off to sleep.

The ability to envision specific details in our projections help us dramatically to understand things that are not yet real. The details become the signs that we are on the path.

What happens though, when every view we have, is bad? They have done studies that show investors in the stock market check their balances more frequently when their money is growing. We are less likely to check the balance of a losing investment. We are wired for good news and naturally recoil from our failures. Everyone writes the book about success but what about the book on failure? We need more talk about the bottom if we want to understand the top.

I went to my attorney one time. I had recently started the One Fire Hot Yoga Festival. It's my largest business failure over the past 10 years. But I am grateful I did it. I started moving the energy, but it wasn't happening fast enough. I brought in two partners. I went to my attorney to help me with the operating agreement. Things were looking like trouble with the partners and the failure writing was on the wall from day one.

Eventually my attorney said to me, "Listen Hargobind. It's like you are trying to paint a Monet. You are thinking pastels. Unique paint colors. You are thinking about your contemporary, Renoir, and the lessons of Boudin. You are taking into account your place in the 19th century impressionist movement. You wonder how the future will see you. And these guys, they are over there eating the paint."

I knew he was right. But after the vision ritual I still had no better option. All options were bad. So I continued forward knowing that even though the partnership was doomed, it was still better than nothing at all. It never made money, but it served a great purpose. When things eventually went south in the partnership, my exercises in vision prepared me for the separation. There was no surprise. Eating the paint was just the meal we ordered.

When I lead dharmify workshops, I emphasize the importance of understanding vision as both an ambition and an exercise in contentment. It's a paradox. On the one hand, you can get clear on what you want. On the other hand, you can flex your contentment muscle. That you are enough. What you are doing is enough.

Shortly after my mother died and reflecting on the transience of life, I went to Mexico City on a one-way ticket. I desperately wanted to enjoy the time I had left. Her passing was tragic yet profound. She died at peace, in my view, like a total spiritual master. She was so fearless and powerful. It wasn't always like that.

My impression of her as a child was that she was scared. My view is that she chose the Sikh path first out of inspiration. She told me that she joined the group because there were so many beautiful people, cool artists and talented musicians. Then they mostly left for various reasons and we were what was left. I think the group inspired her but as the years wore on, she was highly torn about leaving and just felt trapped by the obligations of family and community.

The fear trickled down to me. I was so scared as a kid. I wet my bed until I was 12. I felt so judged and misunderstood by everyone outside our small ashram. Bed wetting causes huge anxiety and fear. Anywhere you sleep, becomes a reasonable source of tension because, well, it stinks like piss. I never changed until I went to boarding school. I realized my classmates would beat the shit out of me if I pissed in their dorm. I stopped wetting my bed almost the day I arrived. Until that point, I was scared of the world, too.

In her late 40's Mom got breast cancer. The reality of death changed her. She became a different woman. She started painting more. She played music more. She got into politics. She organized events. She hosted music festivals. I would come home some days and there would be 100 people in the house singing, chanting, and playing gurbani kirtan. She started traveling as a solo female, to the point that I lost track of where she was. I am proud that our venues cater to solo female travelers. I think they would be a place that she would have loved to visit.

Then 9/11 galvanized her. Balbir Singh Sodhi got shot a few days later in Arizona for wearing a turban. His killer said he was "going to go out and kill some towelheads." She told me that she couldn't tolerate a world that was hostile towards Sikhs for no reason. Especially after raising Sikh children. She would take me to political meetings. She would force me to go introduce myself to politicians. One time she made me introduce myself to Paul Begala and Terry McAuliffe. It is so healthy for a boy to see his mother be somebody other than his mom.

Every week, my mother started coming home with a new message she delivered to Senator Hillary Clinton, or Senator Dick Durbin, or a host of other American politicians mostly Democrat but also Republicans. The wall of her political pictures grew. Her message was that Sikhs were law abiding and the system was failing to deliver on the rights of these Americans. It wasn't enough anymore for Sikh Americans to mind their own business. She felt they needed to actively work for their safety. She started telling everyone what she thought. My uncle Leo, her older brother, was the CEO of Delta Airlines at the time. He told me she called him and told him he wasn't doing enough to protect the human rights of his Sikh and Muslim passengers. After listening, he promised to work on improving Delta's cultural awareness.

My last moments with her were epic. I would massage her feet each night as she slowly lost consciousness. Towards the end, I noticed a softness in her face. The angel of death was close. The connection made me appreciate love like never before. It felt like something was both crushing and jump starting my heart. I would listen to Bill Withers "Ain't no Sunshine When She's Gone" as I ran. I would work a sweat so I could hide the tears as I jogged. My last words to her were that she did such an awesome job and I loved her. I said, "If you need to go, I will be just fine. You did me so right." She was the best mom ever. She died the next morning.

After she passed, I made up my mind to double my efforts to live without fear, be nice and go for it always. I would go for it like she did.

The trauma of my loss also became a karma success for the deep lessons it left me with. I was 21. The pendulum will swing on that one forever. I miss her all the time.

I left for Mexico shortly thereafter.

I studied in Queretaro. Then started wandering through Central and North Mexico. I passed through a cowboy festival in Durango. I watched a rodeo and wandered open air, desert markets. I went to a bullfight in a *plaza de toro*. I fell in love with a beautiful surfer girl in Guanajuato. I dodged a mugging in a pool hall in San Luis Potosi. I walked cobblestone streets in San Miguel De Allende. I took the ferry in Morelia. I went to the beach in Topolobampo. I had the most epic train ride through the tunnels at Copper Canyon. I went mostly by bus. Inside.

I was making friends and dodging danger as I went. As my money ran out, I stayed in hostels with dozens of people. I started hitchhiking more and conserving the last of my cash. No real plan and for a time it was amazing. But running out of money got stressful. Living for the moment, lost its life. I accidentally drained my bank account to zero before I reached the United States.

Nearing the border, I was hitchhiking in the town of Los Mochis, in the state of Sinaloa. I got picked up in a white Chevy Suburban by two guys and two girls rolling slow. With hesitation I got in. First thing I noticed was the girls were hot. One had long black hair, a low-cut white tank top with cut arms and a great figure. The guys were most definitely not hot. One had a big belly and a puffy face with a stubble goatee. But he had energy and he was driving. There were a bunch of empty beer cans at my feet. Aluminum crinkled as I got in. The stench of booze filled the air. The mix of sweat, heat, beer and spit from loud chatter hit me like a web. The main guy was shifting his Corona back and forth while he worked the wheel. As we chatted, he was looking back at me as much as he was watching the road. Once I was in, I couldn't get out.

At first, they said they owned a heavy machinery factory in El Paso. They said they had come for vacation, to party, and see their Mexican girlfriends while their family was back North. Always curious, I started asking about the intricacies of their business when the vibe changed like a strike on the Jethadar. They got serious and the mood went south. They clarified that they were *narcotraficantes* not mere mechanics. The conversation then turned on me. The implication began that with the American passport, I could help them. They dropped me at my hostel to get changed. We agreed to meet later that afternoon at the bar. But it was an order, not an invitation.

I went to the ATM and prayed. The machine spit out cash. I have never been so happy to see money. Unbeknownst to me, I had a cash advance set up, tied to a credit card I didn't know existed. I bought a bus ticket and ran to the station. I crossed back to the USA at Ciudad Juarez, standing up the *carteleros*. The anxiety of the moment made me commit to planning.

The paradox of the present moment is that only by planning for the future, and resolving our past, can we enjoy the now. They have done studies that happiness is derived not from doing what you like, but by being present while doing what you like. Without mastery of the past and future, I would argue it's impossible to be present.

This is another reason I dharmify. So I can use my vision of the future to enjoy and relax in the present.

Vision should at times scare you. I met the second richest man in the world once. At the time, Lakshmi Mittal pegged a net worth of 48 billion putting him just behind Bill Gates on the Forbes list. I gathered the courage to introduce myself to him because of my failed vision and in doing so I got a nice piece of advice. I was returning from my tsunami relief mission and I was stranded in Delhi for a week. I was staying at a seedy cheap hotel on the Delhi outskirts.

I decided to attend a conference with a bunch of Indian luminaries hosted by the magazine, *India Today*. I could either stay at a luxe hotel or stay at a dump and pay for the conference with the last of my cash. Experiences always win for me. The president of Afghanistan was there with his cadre of American mercenaries. Spiritual leader Sri Sri Ravi Shankar debated a film score maker. Amitabh Bachan was there. Senator Hillary Clinton was there, too, and gave a nice speech

I came up with a totally crazy pitch. For some reason, all the planes from Delhi back to the United States were cancelled. I needed to get back before I got in trouble like I did in Mexico. I knew Senator Clinton was flying back the next day. So, I gathered the courage to go introduce myself and explain that I was on a relief mission. I would ask for a ride back on her plane. As

I walked up, I totally chickened out. My palms got sweaty. I started to shake a little. I never introduced myself. I never said a single word. There were tons of people around and none would have known that in my mind I had a real vision. She left. I went back to slump at my table when I noticed Lakshmi Mittal sitting at the VIP table with a free moment.

I loved his talk too. He spoke about the steel industry. He spoke of being an Indian immigrant in China and Indonesia. He spoke of how being different was his advantage. In his home country of India, he wasn't well received. He was one of many. Abroad though, he was different. So, he set out to change the steel industry in foreign lands. If I hadn't chickened out with Senator Clinton, I would have never mustered the courage with Mr. Mittal. I noticed Mr. Bajaj, another scion of Indian business, left his seat and I went and sat in it. I introduced myself to Mr. Mittal and told him I too wanted to change an industry just like him. He asked me which one and I said I wasn't sure. He said pick one and wished me all the best. I left feeling like less of a chicken because I had high vision and pondered what industry would be for me. I shot for the stars but landed in the clouds. To do it right though, we need to chop wood and carry water. Then our full visions become real.

CHAPTER FIVE:

CHOP WOOD, CARRY WATER

Before enlightenment, chop wood and carry water. After enlightenment, chop wood and carry water.

- Zen Koan.

Shit or get off the pot.

- Unknown

Ambitions suck without a calendar

- Brendan Bruchard

In the wild, there are two types of male monkeys that get laid and reproduce. For years researchers thought all monkeys were the product of the dominant male alpha monkeys and their harems of female counterparts.

Alpha monkeys were easy to spot. They were physically bigger. They were stronger. They controlled the resources and the females fawned to them for security and status. The other males knew to keep their distance for fear of incurring the wrath and pounding of a more powerful animal.

When anthropologists started to track the genes however, there was another biological story. Most baby primates were the product of the alpha monkeys, but a huge percentage were not. Some other monkeys were sneaking into the gene pool. The social scientists discovered the sneaker monkey. The sneaker monkeys were getting laid too.

Researchers had no idea how this was possible. They set out to observe more closely. What they found was that a whole class of males were adopting more feminine attributes avoiding detection of both the alphas and the anthropologists. Instead of trying to be bigger, stronger, and dominant, they were helpful to the pack. They gathered food. They were nicer to the females.

They worked hard to create harmony. Then when their opportunity arose the males and females got down while the alphas were away. The sneaker monkeys score too.

My first business mentor in India was my English teacher. She took me under her wing when I started The Caf. She taught me to keep two sets of books just as they did in New York, the business capital of the world. The first would show no profit and the second was the real deal. She explained that if I ever let her colleagues, fellow teachers, know how much money I was making they would certainly come take it away, just as they eventually tried to do. Each night after we closed at 9 pm I would go balance my books working late into the night.

Forget making money though, I was lucky to break even. There was so much pilferage, I would spend hours trying to have it all make sense. With the added difficulty of trying to keep two sets of accounting ledgers, it was logistically impossible. It was the first time I realized that complexity is a profit inhibitor. I tossed that idea and genuinely think it's easier to just do things the right way. Still she shared another gem.

There was a girl that I had a crush on. We were good friends and so innocent. It was going nowhere, and I had no skills to take it further. One time, I was with my mentor amidst our business chats and I confided in her how challenging it was to be a boy.

She stopped me and explained every man has got to become a great salesman. I inferred not everyone has the genes to be an alpha monkey, but everyone can be a sneaker monkey.

So, the sneaker monkey I set out to be. When I first started dating my wife, our mutual friend told her "you know he doesn't have any money right?"

Just last week an opponent on the basketball court asked "has anyone ever said you look like the guy from home alone". He meant the sticky bandit and not the cute one. If I wanted to score, I needed to become a sneaker monkey.

So, a salesman I became. My first job in sales was as a telemarketer. I worked for a US company called American Teleradiology. We offered readings of CT scans and MRIs in remote locations at better prices than a hospital could get from a doctor working on sight. My job was to call every hospital in a state and say, "can I talk to a radiologist". My first step was to sneak past the nurses and administrators that would answer the phone. They wouldn't ask anything more, assuming it was a private medical issue protected by HIPPA.

As soon as I evaded the alpha gatekeepers, I would introduce myself looking for a heart-to-heart connection with a doctor that really didn't want to buy from me. Then I would brace for the inevitable rejection. I would make 50-100 calls per day facing rejection 99.9% of the time. In my 9 months as a telemarketer, I closed 1 deal worth $350,000 netting me $17,500. My one client was in Poughkeepsie New York a place I had never been. I knew my old teacher from New York would be proud that I did a deal in the center of the universe. It dragged on so long, I ended up closing the deal from a pay phone at an Oxxo in Mexico in the middle of my first journey there.

Our doctors were licensed in 14 states and I called every single hospital in each state. My first major break came in Kentucky. I was so thrilled to close my first deal only to realize it wasn't a state we were licensed in. There was a miscommunication about that one. I was then tasked with explaining to my new doctor friend, we couldn't do what I had spent months trying to do. I was reminded of the Tibetan yogi Milarepa whose guru made him build a pyramid of rocks only to then make him destroy the pyramid so he would learn humility, perseverance and fortitude.

I soldiered on facing rejection from more than 1000 people. That's a lot of no but by the time I met my wife, I had literally no fear of rejection. I put my sneaker monkey sales skills to work as my mentor suggested.

I met Siri Om in Espanola, New Mexico at a 3HO Sikh Ashram. It was love at first site for me and she doesn't remember a single thing about it.

She was signing people up to read from the *Akhand Path* which is a continuous reading of the Siri Guru Granth Sahib over 72 hours when read in English. I was signing up for 4 slots at a time just to keep her talking when my friend walked in and said, "Ready to go to the airport?" I was flying out that day and had to unwind the deal once again.

Undeterred I knew she was coming to Washington DC with the same friend. They were doing some work for the government and I figured I might see her again. I invited him over for breakfast knowing that to get to work on time, they would both have to come. So it was like a sneaker monkey trap. I made him fresh pancakes with fruit and yogurt. I made hash browns with mushrooms. I made smoothies and presented it all with the best of my ability. My buddy thought I was totally nuts but Siri Om was impressed. Cooking for someone equals at least two abs on the six pack.

We finally hooked up later that year. Our first night out we went dancing until the club shut down. Then we went gambling at an Indian casino and then drove through the mountains of New Mexico. There were better looking guys. There were richer guys. There were guys with more status. There were more alpha monkeys she could have picked. She even tells me, next time, she is marrying for money. But I took the sneaker monkey road. And that path is open to everyone that wants to work. It is open to everyone that wants to chop wood and carry water.

Soul and karma are about spirituality and the past. They are real to us, but we can't prove them. We believe them. But dharma can be proven right now. It is a statement we can read. It is a declaration that we care about something. Other people could read our dharma and make a judgement of whether we are doing it or not. It is more real in a sense. Vision is the future. Chop wood carry water is the bridge from the past to the future. If we are going to make the visions real, then chop wood, carry water is the work we are going to do. Defining the path is the goal.

When Awakenings Coffee failed, I looked back on the work as pointless. I have never needed to know how to make espresso since. I don't want to sell pastries like they make. I don't need that knowledge. When it looked like Casa Om Potomac was failing, it was vastly different. I was over budget. It forced me to let the general contractor go to more profitable work. It also put so much pressure on me to work physical labor because I couldn't hire help. So, I had to work all day every day. It was also embarrassing. My workers could see they were following a guy who made mistakes. Ultimately, I didn't mind because I was doing work that I really wanted to learn.

I acquired skills in painting, framing, concrete forming, deck making, heavy machinery, trenching, drywall repair, as well as basic education in plumbing, sprinkler, fire alarm and electricity. I was also the purchasing manager and general contractor. I had to raise money under duress and convince lenders to give me money despite my overwhelming failure to plan properly. And I had to do this honestly. I raised twice from a local bank and 4 times from private investors. It was a possibility that I would never finish the project. But really it was an exceptionally good idea whose time had come. If I had waited, it wouldn't have been such a good idea. It was rough, but it would be inevitably worth it. It is exponentially harder to find a great idea than it is to find capital for the idea.

However, if I had to work this hard on a bad idea like Awakenings Coffee, I would be livid. So, this is the difference. Chop wood carry water means win or lose, you are grateful for the experience. That is soul-infused work that leverages our karma. It is a way of thinking about the work we do as a spiritual path in and of itself. It is what we are going to do to make vision real. To make dharma real. With Potomac, I didn't expect to work so hard. If I had better vision, it wouldn't have been so difficult. But we cannot see fully until we reach the end. There is a great movie on this called the Fog of War. It essentially says, in battle we cannot know what's there until the fighting starts. Fog of war is defined in 1896 as "the state of ignorance in which commanders frequently find themselves as regards the real strength and position, not only of their foes, **but also of their friends."**

When I dharmfied for my marriage, it became clear I was overlooking a step. In the vision stage, I said I wanted a great marriage but when I looked at my chop wood carry water, there wasn't much there. I wasn't really doing anything that I could argue was making my vision real. If you say you love someone, prove it. I wasn't breaching the vows we took, but I also wasn't doing the specific things I know to be important to her. When my list came up short, I made 3 distinct changes in my life and added them to my list.

1. Plan a Tuesday date night each week

2. Hire a marriage counselor
3. Buy presents for each major holiday including Christmas, Valentine's Day, our anniversary, and write a heartfelt note on the card each time.

Most people are not doing this type of work. So, when I look at my list now and the time investment I am putting into the marriage, I think I should have a stronger marriage than the people that are not making marriage a priority. I want a marriage that is better than normal because I think most people's marriage leave a lot to be desired. My list is proof that my vision equals my effort. Certainly, it could all still fall apart. We don't control each other. We address that in Guru's Blessing, the last step.

Another area out of alignment was my friendships. Again, when I came to chop wood, carry water here, it was clear I wasn't really doing anything to build my friendships. At this point, friendships aren't so high on the list, but they are important to me. Family, business, and personal health all rank higher right now. When I look at my chop wood carry water here, I am not doing anything though and that's neglect. I am just letting the friendships stall. After reflection, I realized I wanted to do something more.

I started doing a gratitude closing ceremony on my yoga retreats. At the conclusion of the retreats, we send cards to people we are grateful for. Scientific studies show that expressing gratitude increases feelings of happiness in both the recipient and the one who expresses. Putting it into our retreat setting has had exponentially positive effects. It gives me the chance to write my notes to my friends, and shares the process with our guests. Additionally, it leads to an increase in tips for our staff because it allows the clients to reflect on the great service they receive. It's micro-wins all around. So, you can dharmify to improve your friendships and marriage too.

Writing a task list triggers a moment of reckoning.

One of two things will happen next. I generally feel overwhelmed or great. If I feel overwhelmed, this is the best time to be honest with myself. It's like my body senses failure. It has over committed to things in the past. By not listening now, there will be greater pain later. I will let someone else, or myself, down because I don't really want to do it and my body knows it. I can deal with it now by tuning in to my gut instinct and adjust accordingly.

I can always do less. If the vision is too big and I don't want to do the work, then I trim the vision and change the dharma. My whole dharma for a year was to do less. Say "no." Stop working! This constant pressure to live up to the ideas placed in our minds by ancestors, friends, society and ultimately ourselves is often crippling and soul sucking. At this step, here is the chance to reject that which we don't want to do. If the vision does not equal your chop wood, carry water step, then it will hurt. If the soul doesn't overlap with the karma, it will hurt. If dharma creates vision you don't like, it will hurt. If chop wood, carry water is too much to make vision real, it will hurt.

Alternately if I write out my chop wood carry water answers and I feel great, then I get a total hit of adrenaline. I get so excited when I am doing the things that I really want to do. It's 5 am right now and I just got so stoked to work on this chapter. I am so excited about this book that it shot me out of bed. I know my dharma is on point when I am getting hits of excitement coming at me.

When all of these align, it will still be hard, but it won't hurt. It won't exhaust you. It will charge you. It will be awesome.

At any moment though, we can either commit to the work or drop some of the ideas in our vision.

A soccer coach once came and addressed his team. He said to the group, "Tell me about how far you want to go as a team." The team said, "We want to win the state championship! Woo Hoo!!" The coach said, "Great! Last year's champions started practice at 4:30 AM. We too will start at 4:30 AM." The team said, "Well, maybe we want to just be regional champions! Woo Hoo!" The coach said, "Ok great! Last year's regional champions started practice at 6:30 AM. We too will start at 6:30 AM!" The team said, "Well, maybe we will just play club soccer."

Like the soccer team above, measuring your vision to your efforts is liberating. There is nothing wrong with playing club soccer. It's super fun. I used to play six nights a week. But imagine the pain of the coach trying to get his team up at 4:30, when his team just wants to play club soccer.

Lots of people go back at this step and modify the vision. There is so much emotional baggage we all carry regarding what we think our dreams should be. Dropping undesirable ambitions is an important step to finding contentment, the ultimate goal of dharmify.

A few years ago, Kobe Bryant tore his rotator cuff. This is usually a career ending injury, especially at 37. He was asked, "what motivates you to come back?" He said, "The process of it. I want to see if I can. I don't know if I can. I didn't know if I could come back from that [Achilles injury]. I wanted to find out. I wanted to see. What I'm going to do is what I always do, just break everything down to the smallest form, smallest detail, and go after it."

This is the process. You set your vision. In Kobe's case, it was to heal and recover from the shoulder injury. And from there "break everything down to the smallest form, smallest detail and go after it." In our words, chop wood, carry water.

Before we move to the next step, it's worth noting that chop wood, carry water is the first reality check. If you have massive vision but can't possibly execute on it, you will have massive pain. Because you will never live up to your own ambition. This will bring on downward spirals.

I was speaking to a client recently. She is a single mom and high achieving business owner. But her vision is insanely massive. When we got to chop wood, carry water, it was impossible. She couldn't possibly do the work to fulfil the full vision. There weren't enough hours in the day. I asked her how it feels when you don't live up to your expectations of yourself. She said, "I feel terrible." That's it. Why would you want your vision to make you feel terrible? Also, feeling terrible is unmotivating. This makes any level of vision more difficult to achieve. Massive vision without massive means is not strategic. It's cruel.

If you line up chop wood, carry water with vision, then you are in an upward spiral. Your successes will be stepping stones. Alternatively if your vision is too big, you will hate yourself because you aren't living up to your aspirations. We worked on clearing her calendar so she could focus on one massive task. Once she has momentum and micro-wins, we'll up the vision.

Shark Tank investor Mark Cuban is often saying things like, "It doesn't matter how many times you failed, you only have to be right once." Watching him on Shark Tank, I love how focused he gets on companies to just do one thing extremely well. Looking at how our vision lines up with chop wood, carry water is my favorite way to deliver on exactly what's most important while eliminating everything else. As Lebron James often says, we all need to be "keeping the main thing, the main thing."

CHAPTER SIX:
NAPKIN FINANCIALS

"Accounting makes the numbers come alive"

- My grandfather Seymour "Sy" Greenbaum CPA

"Risk comes from not knowing what you are doing."

- Warren Buffett

"A fool and his money are soon parted"

- Proverbs 21:20

The purpose of napkin financials is to answer the questions "Can I do this or not? Am I for real or not?" We want to get to a clear yes or no. In Conscious Selling sales training, they say there are two great answers. Yes and No. The wrong answer is what they call Hopa Hopa land. In Hopa Hopa land, the salesperson is banished to a dystopian world where everyone is thinking about it and never doing it.

In Hopa Hopa land, people are waiting for their boss's approval. Some are talking it over with their spouses. The doormat of a salesperson keeps leaving messages to prospects that never get returned. Still, they are hoping and hoping to get a deal done. The job of the expert salesperson is to either get a yes and win or get a no, so they can move on to a real deal.

Napkin financials is this idea adapted to our dharmas. We want to see if this dharma is a yes, taking me in an upward spiral. Or no, this dharma doesn't have the resources required. In which case, we can go backward and modify dharma or consciously live with the consequences of running into debt. None of us wants to be in this sort of fake hopeful space where we never really do the work to make it happen.

The napkin financials idea largely comes from the myth about the formation of Southwest Airlines. According to the legend, Herb Kelleher mapped out the basic idea for what would become Southwest Airlines on the back of an envelope. He and a partner discussed the details of renting a plane. I imagine they added up how much fuel would cost. How much labor would cost. They added up how many seats they would need to sell. Then they came to a conclusion. This idea would work. Armed with their envelope, they went out and started the most epic airline with legendary service while building a billion-dollar company. I modified the idea for my dharmify purposes because I used a literal napkin a few times.

Napkin financials were extremely helpful to me when building the One Fire Hot Yoga Festival. I did it on a napkin with Herb Kelleher on my mind. I had the concept of inviting senior teachers in the Bikram yoga community together at a festival location with yoga, food and music.

My motivation was I couldn't take getting together with my Bikram yoga friends to hear them all complain about Bikram. There was just so much joy, knowledge and wellness with this group. But it was getting lost. I got into hot yoga because it was fun. I was no longer having fun. I wanted something new. The complaints were valid, but I saw no healing happen once the group just kept repeating the same stories of pain over and over again. I fundamentally believe we all need to express our pain. We need to identify our problems. We need to speak truth to power. I am all in on that. Then the path to healing is through creative problem solving and pursuing great ideas. Repeating and complaining about our pain is vision without chop wood, carry water.

I started to review my karma. I had festival planning experience with Sat Nam Fest. I knew how to book presenters, vendors and build a work exchange team. I had website development experience and I knew Eventbrite. I liked my karma in this space. I merged karma and soul to create a dharma for the festival. I wanted to put on a high-quality hot yoga festival experience that would change the conversation. There would be structured discussions to address real problems. And then the sessions would end. It would bring the discussion back to why we all were together: to practice. I wanted to bring the conversation to healing through yoga.

I went into the vision. I saw that this would make me a better teacher if I could take all the classes offered at the festivals. I would generate good karma. I would meet new friends. I liked the vision.

I went to chop wood, carry water. I would work a lot of long days. Festivals are pretty grueling, like 16-to-18 hour days. There is a ton of prep work. I was game.

Then I went to step 6, Napkin Financials. I scribbled numbers on a white dimpled napkin. I had a problem. I didn't like what I saw.

After estimating my revenues and my expenses I presumed I would lose $30,000. It didn't look good on my rough calculation. I didn't have that kind of dough to lose. So that wasn't possible. I had come too far to lose money on my ideas. I went back to vision. I had to trim it back. We didn't need so much so fast. Generally, you can build slow and cheap, or fast and expensive. I changed the venue from a campground to one of our studios. For housing we rented a hotel up the block. It became an "urban" yoga festival rather than a traditional get-away experience like Sat Nam Fest.

The first One Fire was a packed event in Bethesda, Maryland. We joked it was the greatest gathering of yogis in the history of Bethesda because it was the only gathering in the history of Bethesda. We ended up making a small profit. It is always better to pack a venue than get too big a space and it feels empty. So the quality was better because it was smaller and cozier. It is the nightclub effect. The napkin financial led me to the right execution of dharma. It got me to the right size vision and the right size venue. In a way, I was also dharmifying my community by doing what I could to improve it.

When I am working for money and purpose, it can be confusing to balance the two motivations. What I appreciate about money is that it's a gauge for how well I am serving the market. It means the market is appreciating my efforts by giving me my resources back. Assuming I get soul right, when I am getting paid well, I am aware that I am fulfilling my purpose. When I am struggling financially, it often means I am not impacting the space. My efforts are not reaching the right place. With the first One Fire, making a little money was a strong confirmation that the marketplace wanted what we had to offer. Especially after thinking I was going to lose money. The process was a strong confirmation that the product was good.

The next major insight I have received with Napkin Financials is on the personal level. Lots of people are telling me health is a priority. Or marriage is a priority. Or their family is a priority. I say: show me the money. If you say your kids are important, how much money are you investing into the things that are building your family like counseling, vacations, books to read together, or other items that are known to bond people. If you say you want to get ripped, I say, how much money are you spending on 1 on 1 personal training, your gym membership, massage and your sexy gym clothes. If you are not dedicating a budget to invest in the things that are most meaningful, I think you are lying to both of us. Napkin financials should have line items that show how much money will be spent to make vision real. If you aren't investing in dharma, the right way, you're investing in the wrong way.

One of my neighbors in Puerto Morelos, Mexico, is a politician and major developer. He comes from one of the five main families that built Puerto Morelos and he owns huge amounts of the town. One day we were chatting about a beach clean-up plan we put together. We spoke for about 30 minutes. We talked about a budget. We talked about different tractor options. We talked about global warming of the oceans that caused sea grass to grow more quickly. We talked about the environmental impact of dumping seagrass in the jungle.

We also joked about the Miss Universe pageant, where Steve Harvey crowned the wrong beauty queen. Harvey had it perfect until it came time to choose the winner. It was super embarrassing to go through the whole show and pick the wrong winner in front of millions of people on live television.

We were very thorough, and I was happy to hold such a vast conversation in my ever strengthening Spanish.

So we came to the end of the conversation and said "OK. *Excelente.*" Then it hit me. I was totally lost. "Were we doing the plan?!" I said. After half an hour, I lost him at that key moment when my Spanish failed me. "Which choice was it?" I was paying attention just until the moment that mattered. He said "aaargobeend, you are like Steve Harvey."

Generally after I do a napkin financial, I will write a business plan. But I want to waste no time. I want to constantly be either committing or killing the idea. And I don't want to be the Mexican Steve Harvey because ultimately we want to make the right choice.

My grandfather was an accountant. He used to say accounting makes the numbers come alive. That's the job with napkin financials. We want them to tell us, "Yes! Dharma is on point" or, "No. Modify dharma so the vision changes and then the napkin financials will update."

I know what you're thinking. "Harg, you've screwed up every business you've told us about." And a lot of the problems centered around budgeting poorly.

True story.

Napkin financials have gotten me into so much trouble. At Casa Om Potomac I misjudged my budget by $350,000. That was a massive mistake. I budgeted $500,000 and went over by almost 75%. Some amount of overrun is expected but that really is a massive mistake.

I will take you inside my decision making. First of all, you try to build a retreat center in America in less than 9 months with less than a million bucks. We'll see how far you get. (Do I sound defensive :) ?) Here was my logic. The timing was right. There were no hot yoga retreat centers in the United States. There were very few retreat centers in the DC area. I had $500,000! For the first time in my life, I had capital after selling our studios. I have been business minded since I was building The Caf in India at 14. It took me 20 years to get that much capital. It was the best idea that I had. I had the market. I already had clients going to my property in Mexico. I could sell them on the idea of a summer retreat center. I had the experience. I had the leadership. I had soul + karma + dharma + vision. I had some capital, just not quite enough.

When I looked into the crystal ball, all that was missing was more money. I decided to go for it because I had enough of the pieces in place. I know we never get all the pieces in place and maybe if I waited for the capital, the competition would crowd out the space. Good ideas never last long, and the chance to be first is gold.

It was so painful. I am not going to lie. Raising capital under pressure is not fun. I did things I wasn't proud of. I sold trees off my property. I literally logged the 27 most beautiful trees on the property and felt so much shame in doing so. I got $2700 and two truckloads of stone to pave the driveway we had destroyed with dump trucks. I felt like a real life Settler of Cataan trading wood for stone. As a lifelong vegetarian, I reluctantly traded a deer to an electrician for work. He installed the hot room heater and later went out and shot a deer with his rifle to get paid. I remember the gun shot vividly. I negotiated ridiculously hard with some of my contractors. One no longer speaks to me.

One of my workers saw how much trouble I was in and offered to work for free to help. It brought me to tears. I cried in front of her. I had hard conversations with my family. It's a peculiar situation to find yourself with a beach house in Mexico and an estate on the Potomac River, yet you are financially trapped. During this time, as I mentioned earlier, the IRS notified me that they would revoke my passport. I had sold out our retreat for New Years in Mexico. The US government got furloughed at this time so the IRS would take no calls. I went to the airport not knowing if they would let me onto the plane. I borrowed money from my father-in-law on the way to the airport to pay my chef to feed the group that week. I mean, it was bad.

But this was my path. I saw that I was underfunded, but if I waited, I may never get this close again. So, I went for it. To have this process done first, I could look at no one but myself for my problems. I chose this. I owned this. All the criticism leveled at me and that I leveled at myself was true. But I got Casa Om Potomac built. We did $30,000 last month and booked out 21 out of 30 days. We have almost all 5-star reviews on Tripadvisor and Airbnb. It's the only hot yoga retreat center in the United States. I am crushing it even in the pandemic while social distancing and adhering to CDC guidelines. So that story is true, too.

Without going through the pain, I don't think I could have been any wiser. Everyone can criticize and a few people can do it. Even less people have done it. It's really easy to never do anything and criticize the methods of those who do.

Speaking of imperfect, my favorite TV show character of all time is Gus Fring from Breaking Bad. I liked Gus because he felt like a yogi to me. He seemed like a character from the Bhagavad Gita. In the Gita, Arjuna listens to his Guru Sri Krishna talk about finding purpose amongst war and getting trapped into fights he didn't really want. Sri Krishna gives him the courage and rationale to fight. I could imagine Gus made a deal with his God and it took him to the dark side too. But even though he fell from righteousness, he was still calm. He was deliberate.

He was fearless. He was relentless. He did seva at the police department. He was humble enough to clean tables at Pollos Hermanos.

If I aspired to be a drug kingpin, I would want to be like Gus.

Then I met Gus Fring. The actor Giancarlo Esposito showed up on one of our retreats. He came to Casa Om Mexico! Giancarlo is a real yogi! We did Ashtanga and Bikram and Kundalini and meditation. I knew it! I could see it in his poses and in his meditation. I saw it in the way that he showed up. He is a very special actor and human. Then, at the end of the retreat, Giancarlo paid me a single compliment. He said, "Hargobind, you are a doer."

If you get napkin financials right and chop wood carry water right, then you are a real doer too. Let's do the work!

I am going to make some assumptions about your dharmas. Most people that want to improve their lives are working in at least one of six categories: clarity, health, love, business, family and community.

I've dharmified in my workshops with probably 300 people and overwhelmingly the most common theme is clarity. I hear things like "my dharma is to find my dharma". That's probably 20% of the participants. The remaining dharmas are spread out in the rest of the areas. For the napkin financials, let's assume everything is important and your priorities will be revealed based on how you use your resources. My hope for you is that how you spend equals your dharma.

It is not important how much you are spending. It is not important whether you are a socialist who has renounced the capitalist system or you are a billionaire with money to burn. What's insightful here is when you see the activity and dollar amount, you will see what your priorities are. Include bartering as well if that's a major source of your resource consumption. If there are discrepancies between your investments and your dharma, you will have pain and I suggest you get them in line.

If the napkin financials deliver your vision and support your chop wood carry water, then we are ready for the last step.

CHAPTER SEVEN: GURU'S BLESSING

"One universal creator. True name. Creative being. No fear. No hatred. Undying. Beyond birth. Self-illuminated. ***By Guru's Blessing****"*

- From Guru Nanak's Japji

"The statesman's task is to hear God's footsteps marching through history, and to try and catch on to his coattails as he marches past."

- Otto von Bismarck

"The more I practice, the luckier I get."

- Arnold Palmer

I got enlightened at the Golden Temple but not the way other people do. I was in the middle of a 40-day seva when it hit me like a punch. Each morning I woke at 2:30 AM so I could be on site by 3:30 AM. I was swinging buckets into the *sarovar*, the holy tank of water that surrounds the temple. The Darbar Sahib sparkled in the background. There are sevas inside the temple for baptized Sikhs, but I gravitated to the ones outside, open to everyone. It was my favorite seva. I had a rhythm of scooping to get the buckets out of the pool, filled with water, and into the devotees' hands without spilling on them. I would stand shin deep in the cold water and work up a nice sweat as I repeated my mantra *Sat Nam Waheguru*. Between rhythmic breathing, and loud chanting I would hand water to my fellow sevadars with gusto. Pilgrims would use the water to wipe the marble floors in the predawn hours. It was cold, refreshing and my favorite way to start the morning in my teen years in India.

I was part of a great system of service doing my job with the community when I realized I was carrying a heavy burden. I was ready to unload.

I had to take a massive dump. I plotted my escape to the squatter when I realized I had no toilet paper. In India, they had a saying: eat with your right, wipe with your left but I wasn't there yet.

Until that point, I hadn't dropped the American addiction to toilet paper. I had meticulously packed the white gold and carried it everywhere I went, lest I get caught with my pants down.

I abandoned my post and slid across the wet marble in my foot skis, making it to the squatter just in time. I looked over my shoulder like an immigrant ready to cross the last border.

The first time you wipe your ass with your hand you observe a few things. First, the poop slides up and down your hole like a slip-n-slide until you are squeaky clean. With toilet paper you never really know. Second, your fingernails can scratch your sensitive areas, so you need to tighten your fingers so just the soft part of your finger tips do the work. It reminded me of my slap attack. Instead of toilet paper there is a faucet within reach of the squat or a small bucket that you fill with water to assist in your clean up.

So I did it like everyone else did it. Instead of feeling disgust, I changed my mind and did it so I could get back to seva. Instead of trying to hold it until I got somewhere else or searching in a panic for some weird contraption to wipe with, I got the job done. I did more with less. I washed my hands with soap and checked my fingernails. I smiled at my micro win and went back to my post and finished my seva. This was Guru's Blessing for that day. I had one one less item to worry about everywhere

I went after that. So while the holy endeavors were special the breakthrough came in an unexpected way.

There were many days of seva, but this is the one I remember most.

Guru's Blessing means we only control what we can control and when we do that we get blessed with the next level of wisdom. This is mostly out of our control but totally out of our control when we are actively messing ourselves up. Dharmify gives the tools for finding our most epic alignment so we get lucky more often.

The Sikh religion teaches God is within. So, the words from Guru Nanak's Japji, also detail the elements of our potential from within. That we too are part of the universal creation. We can find a place of no fear, no hatred and transcend beyond fear of death. But still, it is by Guru's grace. Whether Guru Nanak means a guru of the past, a living guru, or the Waheguru, which is the supreme teacher, I don't know.

What I do know is this is the luck factor and alignment is the luckiest way.

There is an element of risk. What if I don't get blessed? What if I don't get lucky? When I dharmify, I recognize that I can get soul, karma, dharma, vision, chop wood, carry water and the napkin financials right, and still totally fail. Your mission is still at the mercy of Guru's Blessing. An element from the outside that can push us either direction. So, the system is no guarantee. What it does though is puts me fully in control of the things that I can control. My job is to get the steps right and then have faith. The more often I align the steps in small ways, the greater my faith becomes. The system flexes my faith muscle through micro wins. So, I am actively increasing my faith.

This is why dharmifying is different from goal setting. Because we put front and center the knowledge that we get very little control on how this plays out. But we have some.

In the book *You Win in the Locker Room First,* the author NFL coach Mike Smith, makes a pretty succinct argument. Every American football team wants to win the Super bowl. That's their goal. We know 31 teams will fail and 1 will win. So, everyone is working for a limited opportunity. A Super Bowl championship is out of the majority of the players' control. Instead, Coach Smith argues that the players should do it the right way. By focusing on what they can control. In each of their respective ways they can contribute. Some can focus on toughness. Some can focus on strength or speed or the fundamentals of play in each game. Focusing on winning the super bowl doesn't breed the habits required to actually win the Super Bowl. I look at Guru's Blessing in a similar way.

Yogananda tells it like this in Autobiography of Yogi. The story is about a guru and his disciple. The student does everything he can perfectly. He gets married. He cares for his family. He runs a modest business. He fulfils his spiritual duties. Still there is one last desire, and it is for a palace. So the guru appears. With his magic powers, the guru manifests the palace to break the student's last attachment. So my take away from the story is the same. We can't do it alone and there are factors beyond our control involved.

So the question becomes how do we set up to get the guru's blessing?

Obviously do the first 6 steps, but there is one more extremely important move.

To set us up for maximum blessing, we look at who or what we are positively impacting through our dharmas.

So, here is my last step.

I look back to my dharma and ask who benefits?

If I execute this plan, who wins?

Then I write the names down. If my lists are super long, I know I will have so much support along the way. If the lists are short, I know I will face tremendous resistance. That's not necessarily bad, it's just going to be hard.

In strictly business terms, as Seth Godin would put it, "this is your smallest viable market. It's the smallest group of people you would have to convert to your cause to succeed".

When I was dharmifying the Casa Om Potomac project, I started writing out name after name of people that would come to host retreats here. This list became extremely important as I doubted myself and ran out of money. Halfway through, I considered flipping the house and just taking a major loss.

The list gave me hope. It kept reminding me that I was working for guru's blessing. I just had to get open so I could be of service to my people. My dad kept saying "if you build it they will come". I would reply, "Papa, that's a fucking movie about ghosts!" But he was right, and he knew it.

Guru's Blessing becomes a gauge as to whether you are succeeding or not. If the people on the page are not buying your services, or they are not happy about your dharma choice, you know you misjudged the market.

At Potomac, I kept thinking about these people that I was working for. They couldn't see what I saw yet. They weren't physically there. The workers couldn't see what I saw. One of my master builders was talking down to me towards the end of the project. He pointed out, "Just because you can build things, doesn't mean people are just going to show up." I was so tickled he thought I was a builder. My list from Guru's Blessing was real. I just had to give it the chance to manifest.

When these lists are long, I know I just need to get there. I have 200 people on my Guru's Blessing list for this book. I am so stoked to get it done and share it with them.

When I was dharmifying my marriage, I put down the names of my close family. If my wife and I are happy, my daughter benefits. She even tells me she doesn't like when we argue. My in-laws benefit. Our employees benefit. Our mutual friends benefit. And I really benefit. I am so happy to put the effort in because these people that are close to me keep showing up on the path. I love that. I don't want to let down all these people. That would be so sad.

I have messed up Guru's Blessing a ton of times.

I started a website one time called ratemyyogateacher.com. It's so embarrassing. I invested $2000 into it. I worked with my buddy on coding it. I launched it. I was thinking "how is it possible to start a dialogue with as many yoga teachers as possible?" It seemed like a way to create a database. I was selling yoga books and CD's at the time. So, I did it. Total flop. Totally useless. I explained to someone with excitement what I was doing. He asked incredulously, "Rape my yoga teacher!?"

No one wanted this. If you don't like the class, why would you want to complain about it on the internet? I had no real customer in mind. I had no real people that would benefit from this. I probably had no soul in it either. I have, to my knowledge, never left anything but a 5-star review online anywhere. I am absolutely the worst guy to build a rating site. I am so positive. I hate arguing online. Clearly, guru did not bless me on this one.

You can use Guru's Blessing for anything. If your dharma is relationship oriented or personal development oriented, getting clear on who benefits will keep you so motivated. Working to provide value to others creates so much positive energy coming back your way.

One of my clients who experienced lots of racism in his life asked me, "Should I put down all the people that are trying to screw me over in here?" Because for him to succeed, he had to overcome lots of people that were actively discriminating against him for his skin color. He put those people on another list. That made me sad for him but it is his reality.

When these lists are long, you will get a lot of support in your dharmas. When they are short, you will face a lot of struggle alone. I like to have long lists of Guru's Blessing. Then as I go through my dharmas, I get a lot of validation when these people show up on the path.

This is the crux of the argument. We can't predict victory. We shouldn't expect failure. The best we can do is create epic alignment. When soul plus karma creates dharma, vision is triggered. If we are game to do the work in chop wood, carry water, and the napkin financials are a yes then we have momentum. If the Guru's Blessing is on point, then we are on the most epic spiritual path possible.

We can't control the Guru's Blessing. However, we can set up everything to give ourselves the best chance. That's what I hope for you. Get the dharmify right and you've done the absolute best you can.

Conclusion

I am the happiest, most content, most ambitious, most focused, and healthiest version of myself that I have ever been. 2020 - despite the pandemic, getting hit by two hurricanes at Casa Om Mexico, halting business, quarantining, and homeschooling - has been the best year of my life because I have been dharmifying daily. More than any other time in my life, I have taken the time to systemically do what's most meaningful most days.

My highest hope for this work is the word "dharmify" gets adopted into the common vernacular. The more we clarify what matters most, the more we can do what matters most. Massive shifts in society are occurring right now from war, unemployment, migration, and pandemic-related crises *as usual*. This is not a special time in history and in the context of historical crises, we aren't that special either. However, we are vested with the power to fix ourselves and in doing so, have a positive impact on the Earth around us. We are the most powerful humans to ever walk this planet and that is unique. It is simply all that we can do. Beyond that, it's Guru's Blessing.

I was reading the letters from Indian soldiers enlisted to fight on behalf of the British in World War I in Europe. I was wondering the mindset of someone sent to fight and die for a country that conquered them. How would one find hope, purpose, or make sense of this type of risk? How would one dharmify that life? Some letters wrote of being trapped in endless trenches for days. Others mentioned feelings of hopelessness. Commentary mentioned the soldiers' lack of education. Their lack of alternative means. Some mentioned coming from poverty. They spoke of knee deep mud that consumed them. Bombs of fire falling from the sky. Machine guns that shoot 700 rounds per minute ripping men to shreds. They wrote of carnage and certain death.

But the line that hit me the hardest was this from a soldier to his lover back home, "I am like a soap bubble, and have no hope of life! How many days is it since I was separated from you, star of my eyes. But you must realize that this is the time for brave men."

It was 24 years ago that I was soaked in my blood punching myself in the face. On the one hand positive change is a long journey. On the other hand, there is nothing better to do.

It is always the beginning if you start right now. Give the dharmify a shot with the sheets attached. I recommend you dharmify the long way here and then try the shorter 10 minute dharmify daily. I think you will find it becomes a helpful routine for you to use each day to maximize time spent on what is most important. Then I hope you extend it out to your love life, your business, your challenging family dynamics, your health and beyond.

If I can help you dharmify, find me:
facebook.com/hargobind
@hargyoga on Instagram
Or email me at hargobind@casaom.com

PS: please come visit me at Casa Om Mexico and Casa Om Potomac! We will go all out on dharmify!

Finally, a last request.

If you enjoyed Dharmify: A daily practice to get your mind right, your business tight, be a love light, so you feel alright, please leave me a review on Amazon.com

It would mean so much to me!

Dharmify yourself (the long version)

SOUL

Tell me about your soul.

- What are 3 reasons you are reading this book?
- What are 5 things that you are passionate about?
- What excites you to wake up in the morning?
- What are 5 things that are important to you?
- What, if anything, is holding your soul back?
- What, if anything, do you hate doing that you are currently doing?
- If you could change 3 things in your life, what would they be?

- What, if anything, would improve your intimate relationships?
- What, if anything, would improve your sex life?
- What, if anything, could improve your health?
- On a scale from 1 to 10 with 1 being super discontent and 10 being super content. Where are you?

When I think of an awesome day, it's filled with small victories. I call them micro-wins. Stacked micro-wins create upward spirals. Think of a great day you had.

- What are five things that combined would make a great day for you?

I am trying to stack upward spirals at all times so I can avoid downward spirals.
Think of a bad day.

- What were 5 elements that piled on top of each other to make it that way ?

KARMA

Successes

- What 5 successes have impacted your life most?
- What 5 things are you good at?

- What are 5 things that you have done that have shaped you?
- What educational degrees do you have?
- What 5 traumas have you experienced in your life?
- What, if anything, do you feel holds you back from success?
- What are 3 ways that your family supports you?
- What are 3 things that make you proud of your country?
- What are 3 types of communities that you identify with?
- What are 3 ways that your community enables your success?

Traumas

- What 5 failures stand out for you the most?
- What if any are ways that your community is holding you back?
- What are 3 things that you wish your country did better?
- What, if anything, are ways that your family holds you back?
- What are 5 experiences where you have been ashamed of yourself?
- Who/how have you been hurt?

DHARMA

Here is how you write your dharma. Go back to your soul and karma questions. Look at what are the most meaningful words there. Find the answers with the most energetic charge. Then put it into your dharma statement. My argument is when your path forward is soul infused and resolves karma or builds on yoru success, you will find the most fulfilling path.

My dharma is ____________(use soul words to charge and resolve your karma) ____________________

Here is how I work to create vision.
Imagine we have a time machine. After declaring dharma, we hop one year ahead.

- Looking back, what most notably, has happened in the past year of your life?
- What are 5 things that you have done that stand out for you?
- Who are 3 people that are with you?
- What are 3 locations where the dharma took you?
- Choose one statement: "I like what I have done" or "I don't like what I have done."
- What are 3 things that you are most proud of?

- What are 3 ways that you have resolved your karma?
- What, if any, are your personal problems?
- What goals that you set, have you accomplished?
- Do you like what you see? Yes or no.

Are you content with how you used your time? yes or no
If you aren't content with this vision, go back and change dharma. The insight visioning gives you shows up in how you feel. Your body doesn't understand time like your mind does. When you go into your visions of the future, your body feels certain ways. I love going into my visions and feeling what it's like to travel a particular dharma. Oftentimes I go into my visions and I don't like how I feel. This is the best sign that I am off track with my dharma. Visions should feel epic.
When I start doing chop wood, carry water, I am asking what are all the things I have to do to make vision real.
These are the questions to answer for you to chop wood, carry water:

- If you are going to make vision real what are 5 things that you have to do listed in a task format?
- How much time each day do you have to commit?
- What if any are 3 things that you have to learn?
- What are the 3 most important things you can do today?

If you use Google calendar, I highly recommend you take these 3 things to do today and schedule them onto your calendar. Without accountability for our work and putting it on the schedule, I think we are deluding ourselves. The use of a calendar is the most helpful way for me to keep up with chop wood carry water. Much respect to my coach Satgurmukh for hammering this home with me.

- What are three things you can cut out of your life to make space?

  Now, most importantly!

- Do you want to do that? Hell yes! or…. no?

This is a moment of reckoning.
Here is how I do my napkin financials for an idea over a single year:

Napkin Financials	Year 1	Year 2
Coming in		
Going out		
Margin or loss		

Ok or not Ok

Pick one

Timeframes could be years, months or days depending on what you are trying to achieve but, it's all the same.

I estimate what's coming in. I estimate what's going out. I subtract what's going out and what's left is the margin which can be positive or negative.

Am I good with that? Yes or No.

So this process is raw. It's not thorough. Please dive deeply into budget analysis, a business plan and market research when cultivating your ideas. What's going to happen after thorough study is eventually you come back to this.

Is it on or not? Am I doing it or not? All the thinking eventually boils down this question. Yes or no?

GURU'S BLESSING

- Name 10 people who benefit if you make this dharma happen?
- Specify 3 ways in which this dharma will help them?
- Name 3 people that will try to stop you from living your dharma?
- Is that a problem? Yes or no?

If yes, that's a problem, then go backwards and modify something so it becomes a no.

Dharmify daily (the short version)

Now that you have the basics of the system, I have one more suggestion to make. Try the Dharmify Daily. Try to do it as fast as you can so it is an enhancement of your life and not a burden on your time.

Here is how I do it on the daily. I set a timer for 10 minutes and then start.

SOUL:

What does my soul want today? How do I want to feel tonight?

KARMA:

What karma can I resolve or success can I build upon today?

DHARMA:

What is my dharma and what combo of the 6 categories (health, love, business, clarity, family, community) will guide me today?

VISION:

What is the high vision for the day?

CHOP WOOD, CARRY WATER:

What is my task list?

NAPKIN FINANCIALS:

What resources will I invest today and what is the best way to make the most money today?

GURU'S BLESSING:

Who will benefit from my high vibe living today?

I know that if I don't rate my day 10 out 10 then there is some inauthentic stuff creeping into my day. Try this for a week, and I bet it will become a permanently useful tool to improve your life as it has for mine.

Two more elements that will help with cultivating soul.

1) Make an upward spiral

Include 5-7 things that combine to make a great day for yourself. My observation is that when good things combine its easier to tackle hard but necessary things. Here is my upward spiral.

- Slept well and woke without alarm
- Pranayama 30 breaths x 2 with muscle contraction
- Mantra recitation
- Cold shower
- Got a big deal done at work
- Made popcorn for Siri Om and Siana
- 90 minute handstand practice
- Meditated for 11 minutes at night

My upward spiral

Fill in your upward spirals

2) Make a downward spiral

Next time you have a bad day, deconstruct it and write it here in a downward spiral. You'll see that your feelings, thoughts and beliefs are directly tied to your downward spiral. Then you can use the items in the upward spiral to turn this around if you want. Here's a downward spiral I was in two days ago:
Heard sad news about one of my teachers

- My pops was having a hard day
- Siana was ungrateful for things I did for her
- My wife was busting my chops
- I was low energy
- I didn't make time to dharmify
- A big financing deal at work was falling thru
- I had a big cancellation in Mexico due to covid

All this added up to me feeling sad and like those around me were ungrateful. As I dharmified the next day, I split this into dharmifying how I would move forward with my teacher and how I would get back into an upward spiral. That helped me bounce back to a strong mindset quickly while also acknowledging my problems.

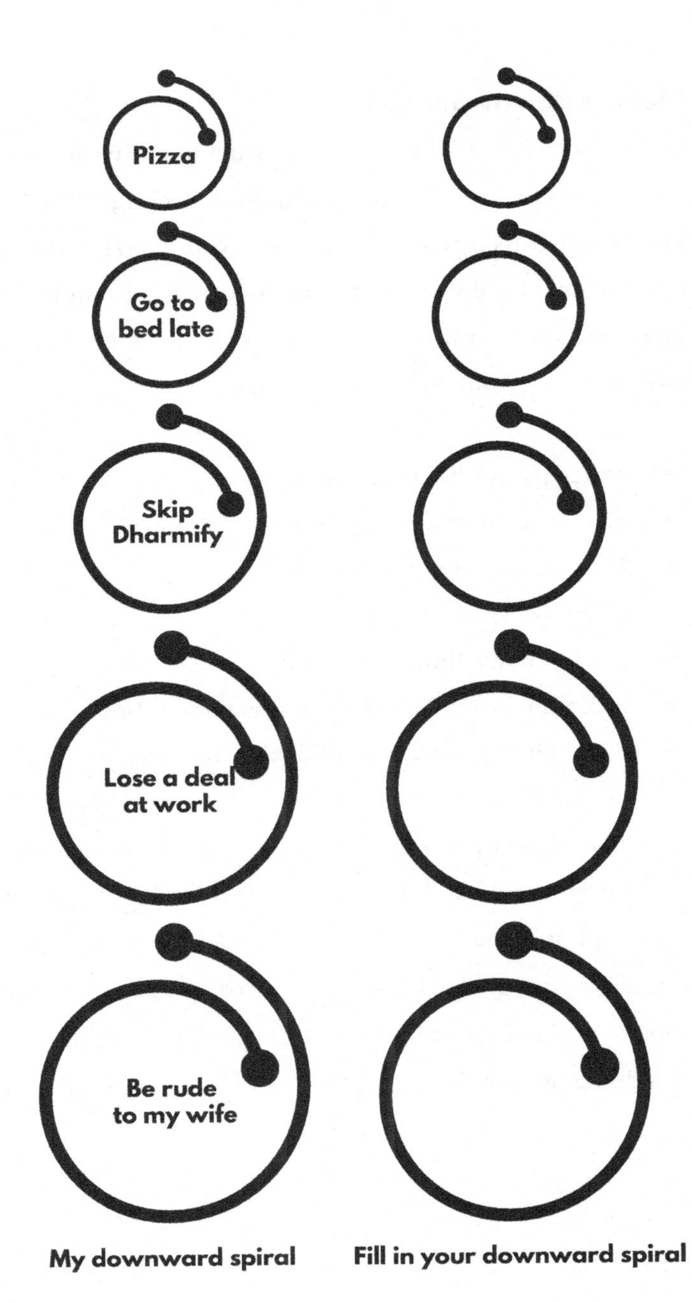

My downward spiral

Fill in your downward spiral

Acknowledgments

This book would not have been possible without the direct contributions of the following people. And forgive me for anyone I left out.

Siri Om Khalsa for being the love of my life and support in this project, Siana for reminding me she just wants to know when its play time, Ann Pallasch for the needed energy at the right time to get this done, Sally Harney for the infinite edits, Rob Hartman for the military strategy and being a brother, Lucille Allen Moran for being a great critic, Tara Ho for all the helpful edits, Robert Swallow for providing help on early drafts, Mallory Shipe for helping me find my voice, Marcus Antebi for helping me zero in on why this is helpful to the reader, John Marcoux for being so damn cool and the best writer I know, Michelle Gano for coaching me, Christos Angilodakis for the artwork, Sat Bir Khalsa for being my bro and providing useful content on the India years, Satgurumukh Singh Khalsa for being a motherfucking yoga master and coaching me in high performance coaching while I wrote this, Sadasatsimran Khalsa for helpful reflections on Guru Gobind Singh and Dharma, Kim Sickmen for being the Casa Om retreat leader G.O.A.T., Tuyet-Nhi for bringing her team to dharmify and the best quote, Prabhjit Singh for insights on gurbani, Michael Clarity for reading later drafts, Satwant Khalsa for being a phenomonal dad and useful edits, Sat Darshan Khalsa for being my big sister always and helpful feedback, Dave Pryor for artwork, Grandma Gloria Greenbaum Cooper for being the matriarch and showing me how to live stright, Lerika Lagarde for running a great property at Casa Om, Stefania Maracas for keeping everything running through thick and thin, Karan Khalsa for being a dope sister, Guruganesha Khalsa for teaching me Conscious Selling, Uncle Joe Mullin for insights on my mother and looking after me even in the Delhi nightclubs, Arezu for her graphic contribution on soul and karma, Amrit Singh Phd for reviewing later drafts, Simran Stuelpnagel for providing helpful reflections, Jamie Greenzweig for edits midway through, Gurmukh Kaur Khalsa whose teaching style influenced me most and for midway draft contributions, Charlie Michelson for coaching me during the early stages of dharmify, Alejandro Martin for formatting, and Ditta for early designs, Jeannine Marzella for relationship insights, Partap Khalsa for historical reflections in West Virginia, and Alyssa Sieb for photography.

Casa Om Puerto Morelos, Mexico

Casa Om Potomac

This was me at around 7 years old

Papa, Mom and I

Looking ready for a gatka match in Anandpursahib 1998

Family

Made in the USA
Middletown, DE
23 January 2024

48006140R00110